A STRANGER'S SUPPER

An Oral History of Centenarian Women in Montenegro

TWAYNE'S
ORAL HISTORY SERIES

Donald A. Ritchie, Series Editor

ZORKA MILICH

A STRANGER'S SUPPER

An Oral History of
Centenarian Women
in Montenegro

TWAYNE PUBLISHERS
An Imprint of Simon & Schuster Macmillan
New York

PRENTICE HALL INTERNATIONAL
London   Mexico City   New Delhi   Singapore   Sydney   Toronto

Twayne's Oral History Series No. 17

A Stranger's Supper: An Oral History of Centenarian Women in Montenegro
Zorka Milich

Twayne Publishers
An Imprint of Simon & Schuster Macmillan
866 Third Avenue
New York, New York 10022

Library of Congress Cataloging-in-Publication Data

Milich, Zorka.
    A stranger's supper : an oral history of centenarian women in Montenegro /
Zorka Milich.
       p. cm.—(Twayne's oral history series; no. 17)
    Includes bibliographical references and index.
    ISBN 0-8057-9131-0 (alk. paper)
    1. Montenegro—Social life and customs. 2. Montenegro—History.
3. Women—Yugoslavia—Montenegro—Interviews. 4. Centenarians—
–Yugoslavia—Montenegro—Interviews. 5. Oral biography. I. Series.
DR1835.M55 1995
949.7'45—dc20   95–21903
                                                CIP

10 9 8 7 6 5 4 3 2 1 (hc)
10 9 8 7 6 5 4 3 2 1 (pb)

Printed in the United States of America

To my daughter, Andrea,
my sisters, Emily, Rose, Mary, and Georgine,
and their daughters,
and to Jovanka, the Mother of us all

Contents

CONTENTS

Foreword

The twentieth century is closing as it opened, with violent conflict in the Balkans. Nationalist movements in that region triggered World War I and have reemerged to inflame the states that formerly made up Yugoslavia. In 1990, just before fighting erupted again, Zorka Milich interviewed women in the remote villages of Montenegro. Some were Eastern Orthodox Christian, others Roman Catholic or Muslim; all were over the age of 100. These women were eyewitnesses to a century of turmoil and inheritors of an even longer history of bloodshed. They recount the blood feuds, vendettas, and endless struggles carried out in the name of tribal honor that claimed the lives of their husbands and sons. The accounts of these women, survivors with communal and personal stories to tell, are vivid testimony to what has made peace in their region so elusive.

Oral history may well be the twentieth century's substitute for the written memoir. In exchange for the immediacy of diaries or correspondence, the retrospective interview offers a dialogue between the participant and the informed interviewer. Having prepared sufficient preliminary research, interviewers can direct the discussion into areas long since "forgotten" or no longer considered of consequence. "I haven't thought about that in years" is a common response, uttered just before an interviewee commences with a surprisingly detailed description of some past incident. The quality of the interview, its candidness and depth, generally will depend as much on the interviewer as the interviewee, and the confidence and rapport between the two adds a special dimension to the spoken memoir.

Interviewers represent a variety of disciplines and work either as part of a collective effort or individually. Regardless of their different interests or the variety of their subjects, all interviewers share a common imperative: to collect memories while they are still available. Most oral historians feel an additional responsibility to make their interviews accessible for use beyond their own research needs. Still, important collections of vital, vibrant interviews lie scattered in archives throughout every state, undiscovered or simply not used.

Twayne's Oral History Series seeks to identify those resources and to publish selections of the best materials. The series lets people speak for themselves, from their own unique perspectives on people, places, and events. But to be more than a babble of voices, each volume organizes its interviews around particular situations and events and ties them together with interpretive essays that place individuals into a larger historical context. The styles and format of individual volumes vary with the material from which they are drawn, demonstrating again the diversity of oral history and its methodology.

Whenever oral historians gather in conference, they enjoy retelling experiences about the inspiring individuals they have met, the unexpected information they have elicited, and the unforgettable reminiscences that would otherwise have never been recorded. The result invariably reminds listeners of others who deserve to be interviewed, provides them with models of interviewing techniques, and inspires them to make their own contribution to the field. I trust that the oral historians in this series—as interviewers, editors, and interpreters—will have a similar effect on their readers.

DONALD A. RITCHIE
Series Editor, Senate Historical Office

Preface

The oral histories of Montenegrin women presented in this book are an outgrowth of my doctoral dissertation, a comparative study of the war fiction of two contemporary Nobel Prize recipients writing on either side of the Atlantic Ocean about two diverse civilizations: Yugoslav Ivo Andrić and American William Faulkner. Researching Andrić in Yugoslavia, assisted by a grant from the Ivo Andrić Foundation in Belgrade, stimulated my interest in nineteenth-century Yugoslav women. Scholarship on Andrić's Bosnian women proved invaluable, but I wanted to know the living history of those women born under oppression, survivors of years of foreign occupation: Ottoman and Austro-Hungarian.

Having no previous experience in oral history, I sought the expert counsel of the late Dr. Albert Bates Lord of Harvard University, who had spent three years in Montenegro. In *The Singer of Tales* (1960), Lord's definitive study of oral epic songs in Bjelo Polje, Yugoslavia, he notes that in terms of the oral tradition "there is none equal to Homer . . . but he who approaches the master most closely . . . is Avdo Međedović of Bjelo Polje" (foreword). His simple and pragmatic advice was highly effective: "Just be yourself. You have a warm, friendly personality, speak the language, have a genuine curiosity about life, so just relax and be yourself." He gave me the confidence I needed to move forward.

My initial plan to compare the lives of Christian and Muslim women in Montenegro—which means "Black Mountain"—and Bosnia was thwarted by time constraints. So rich was the assembly of centenarians in Montenegro that I had no time to work in Bosnia. What I unveiled in Montenegro was life in a methodically circumscribed warrior patriarchy, revealed through the collective social and cultural memory of females more than a century old. The resonance of their heretofore unheard voices pervades this study.

In 1990 I interviewed an undocumented population of 30 illiterate tribal women of Eastern Orthodox Christian, Roman Catholic, or Muslim heritage, all between the ages of 101 and 115. No formal records of their births exist. Rather, birth years are associated with specific wars, campaigns, natural catastrophes (such as earthquakes), or the birth of a male relative, as are birthdays. Some women take as their birthday the nearest patron saint's day. Some are also named after that saint. With two exceptions, the women I interviewed were lucid, articulate, and utterly perplexed that a foreigner—an American at that—had any interest in their simple lives. Had I been there to record the life histories of men, they would have readily understood, for in their world men take center stage. Men are the warriors celebrated in the epic tales the women memorize and recite to their sons. Much as I was interested in talking with the men, I made it clear to these women that I had crossed the ocean and the European continent solely to meet them and to hear them tell their stories. I wanted them to journey into the deep recesses of their memories. And what a journey it was. As one who speaks their language and is the offspring of Montenegrin parents—*gorji list,* or "leaf from the forest"—I was welcomed as if a member of the family. An endearing quality of this society is its hospitality. In the poorest home a guest is royalty, offered the finest the family can provide, even if it means depriving the children of food.

Hospitality among Montenegrins and Albanians living in this region extends well beyond food and shelter. With an ethnologist, a *malesorac* (Roman Catholic Albanian), I visited the remote ancestral village of his birth, where conditions had remained unchanged for hundreds of years. It is only within the last 20 years that his people have abandoned their villages, settling in Tuzi, a town on the periphery of the capital city of Podgorica (formerly Titograd) inhabited by Christian and Muslim Albanians. While in his village I visited some of the old, abandoned stone houses. I found it peculiar that my guide never left my side, even for a moment, carefully instructing me where to walk and how to stoop under fences to avoid injury. During our ride home, he explained that while in his company I was under his protection; even the slightest mishap would have disgraced him. In *High Albania* (1971), Edith E. Durham relates an experience from her adventure during the early years of the twentieth century. A man had given her drinking water from his house, and because she accepted it, she became his guest. He was now "bound by his honour to avenge me," she writes, "should anything happen to me before I had received hospitality from another" (32).

Another Albanian told me an incredible story of hospitality in its extreme form. A group of young men engaged in an altercation in which one man was killed. With a posse in pursuit, the killer slipped into a house. The head of the household stood on the threshold, prohibiting the young men from entering. When they revealed that the man hiding in his house had just murdered his son, he calmly responded, "He crossed my threshold, and while he is under my roof he is my guest, and no harm will come to him. So go home, all of you." After several days of providing food and safe lodging for the young man, the father asked him how much time he needed to go home, pack his things, and leave town. "Three days," the young man responded. "I will give you four days to leave town," replied the father. "Just remember, I will be looking for you, and when I find you, I will kill you." He then escorted the killer safely out of the village, still bound by the strict tradition of hospitality. Rumor has it that the young man fled to the United States, though it is doubtful he will be any safer here than in his own country.

Blood revenge, though outlawed, remains a clandestine practice in this culture. Had the young killer exercised more self-control, a chain of tragedies could have been prevented: the death of a youth in the prime of life; the imminent death of the murderer; two grieving families denied sons and brothers; another death when the murderer's family seeks to avenge their son. And so the cycle continues, until one or both families decide the score has been settled. During the six months I spent in this part of the world, I heard many such stories. My son, Mark, a filmmaker, who videotaped a number of my interviews, also taped the funeral of a young man killed in a situation similar to the one just related.

I came to Yugoslavia to conduct my study in January 1990 and stayed until July 1990. Once settled into a previously arranged furnished apartment, I began to search for my subjects. I contacted the History Institute of Montenegro in Podgorica, as well as historians and academics with whom I had communicated earlier, who kindly offered their time and expertise. Despite my enthusiasm, I suspect some were as baffled about my project as were the women I came to record. They nevertheless offered any assistance within their purview. Their generous guidance and incredible fount of information overwhelmed me. No words can adequately express my eternal gratitude.

Considerable preparation remained prior to entertaining the notion of a first interview, to say nothing of actually doing it. I knew my informants were out there. But where? How will they know I am looking for them? How will they know I am here? My own great-grandmother lived well past a century. Nor was she an isolated case, as my mother tells me. "*Crnogorke*" (Montenegrin women), she says, "are condemned to live long, painful lives. My Baba [grandmother] Andjuša believed that all women were cursed; otherwise what else could explain such suffering for so long?"

Dr. Branko Kostić, then president of the Republic of Montenegro, turned out to be my lucky star. Never having met a president of a republic, I hardly knew how to behave nor what to say. To say I was embarrassed and intimidated verges on understatement. That day I truly learned that desperate acts are indeed the consequences of desperate circumstances. Quelling my pride (a Montenegrin, if anyone, would know what agony that entails), I was ushered into his office by a gracious secretary. After initial introductions, we sat, not in any formal way, but rather on a sofa in an unobtrusively furnished room. I related the specifics of my parents' tribal ancestry and the mythic pull of history that had drawn me to the Black Mountains, so saturated with tragedy and courage. I also learned about his clan and its relationship to that of my parents. I then experienced the traditional hospitality of Montenegro in Dr. Kostić's offer of coffee or juice. Montenegrin hospitality was far from new to me, but receiving it in the office of the president from the president himself was incredibly moving.

Feeling infinitely more at ease and my emotions securely under control (restraint being a given in the life of any Montenegrin, native or otherwise), I detailed the nature of my mission. President Kostić was genuinely pleased that my study would make a significant contribution to the world's knowledge of a little-known population. His first comment, "How can Montenegro facilitate your research?" dispelled even more anxieties. For the first time I felt more than a glimmer of hope that my fieldwork would be successful. In my presence he telephoned the director of TV Titograd, stating my objective, and personally arranged a meeting, leading to my being interviewed on prime-time television. When Dr. Kostić understood that I had no transportation, he enlisted his secretary to place a car and driver at my disposal. His parting words, "Whatever other assistance you might need, feel free to call this office and speak to me. What you are doing is also good for Montenegro," unhinged me, and I embraced him.

That evening, when reviewing the events of the day, I felt somewhat embarrassed by my exuberant behavior. I have no recollection of my feet touching the ground as I walked out of the president's office and onto the street. The light was no longer at the end of the proverbial tunnel. It was here. Immediately following my appearance on television, people (many men and one woman) proudly offered the names and locations of their 100-year-old mothers, grandmothers, and great-grandmothers. Further interviews with several journalists produced newspaper and magazine articles about my work, resulting in still more contacts. I had not had even one name at the start. Preliminaries now firmly in place, I began making appointments with these soon-to-be "historiographers"—female voices speaking across time, holding up a mirror to the past.

Those who volunteered the names of proposed narrators made the appointments with their respective candidates. They also accompanied me on the interviews. Without these contacts—whom I shall call coordinators—I could not have accomplished what I did in the limited time afforded me. The moment I was contacted I hurriedly arranged transportation. On the way to our destination, the coordinator, the driver, and I discussed our respective backgrounds and families, my Montenegrin connection, and—always—history. Montenegrins are renowned for their finely honed rhetorical skills. Words flow freely, particularly when the subject is politics—past, present, or future. Montenegrins' history, painful and violent to be sure, defines them as individuals and as a people. Though reserved among strangers, Montenegrins are a remarkably social and verbal people, with a dry sense of humor and a gift for metaphor. As with all other emotions, laughter is consciously controlled, as though an expression of joy would weaken or negate their eternal struggling. I don't recollect hearing a hearty laugh while there, unless I forgot to remember my place.

Once we arrived at the home of my narrator, usually around midmorning, we were welcomed in front of the house by our host (head of the household) and a fairly sizable group of male relatives. Montenegrins live in extended families. Sons, married or otherwise, live at home, as do unmarried daughters. Thus, three married sons with families can increase the size of the household considerably. We were then escorted into the house by the host, and the women kissed me three times, as is customary. Introductions by a third party are not a Montenegrin tradition. All guests are expected to shake hands with everyone present, including children, while introducing themselves. The host, however, introduced me personally to the central figure of the day, my narrator, the embodiment of nobility, whom I kissed according to tradition. I presented her with several pounds of coffee, which the family would later roast and grind for thick demitasse. (Use of the third-person singular pronoun when referring to my narrators is deliberate and appropriate, for their clothing, their behavior, and the stories they tell are derivative of a collective experience and a collective conscience.)

No sooner did the men and I sit down than our host served us homemade *šlivovica* (100-proof plum brandy) or *loza* (brandy distilled from the mash of pressed grapes). While we were toasting one another, the women, who had discreetly slipped into the room behind us, placed on the table homemade cheese (goat and/or sheep), *skorup* (a type of very soft cream cheese), freshly made yogurt, *pršuta* (heavily smoked ham, sliced thin), and bread hot out of the oven. Excluding my narrator, none of the women entered the living room, except to replenish the food. Instead, they remained in the kitchen, within sight, overseeing and listening to the conversation, though rarely contributing to it.

Following an hour of socializing with the family, the host escorted my narrator and me to a private room, obviously selected in advance, where the interview took place. Before departing, he informed her of the reason for my being there, though it is doubtful she was not fully aware of it. He also suggested she respond to all of my questions as frankly and explicitly as possible. When I interviewed a woman who lived on a *katun* (summer pasture), where a house may consist of only a single room, everyone went outside while we remained indoors. To allay any anxiety, the host also reminded her that so important was she that I had come from America just to talk with her. There was never a moment when I sensed she was not in complete control.

Alone with my narrator now, I took several minutes to set up the recording equipment while she silently observed my every move. In the few seconds before the interview, I also carefully noted her. Before me sat a very alert, elderly woman as "to the manner born": imperial, confident, and proud, hands clutching a neatly folded handkerchief in her lap. In her eyes, gentle yet penetrating, lay the cumulative wisdom born of centuries of naked toil and agony in an androcentric environment. To say I was humbled is to barely express my awe.

She would be wearing either all-black clothing or national dress, the one in which she was married and wore for special occasions, which would ultimately become her burial dress (Muslim women wore their traditional apparel). Her attire was immaculate, as was she; her daughters-in-law or granddaughters-in-law saw to that. A black kerchief, tied in the back, covered her hair. Amazingly, none of the women had totally white hair. Whether a subject was feeling discomfort, fear, or embarrassment was impossible to discern. What she exuded was total resignation. There was a job to be done and she would do it, consistent with the pattern of her life: life is what it is, and to question or to complain is pointless.

Once the interview was completed, I photographed her with a professional camera and a Polaroid camera, presenting her with the instant copy as a memento of our time together. To protect the identity of the women quoted in this study while they remain alive, I do not use their photographs or their real names in this book. To protect their identity as well, the women whose photographs appear in this book have not been quoted. How gratifying it is to know that future generations will have the unique opportunity of hearing the voice of a century-old woman speak the dialect of her ancestors, sharing her life as she perceived it. All translations to English are my own.

The reader is undoubtedly curious about the longevity of women in a land as impoverished and harsh as Montenegro. Although in recent years much has changed, these centenarian women spent a good part of their lives as their ancestors did. Is the type of food they ate a factor? The selection depended on the season. In winter the basic diet consisted of beans, cabbage or kale, and potatoes boiled with whatever smoked meat was available. Fresh meat was reserved for special celebrations, such as a wedding or *slava* (clan patron saint's day, passed down patrilineally), at which time lamb and/or pigs were slaughtered and roasted outdoors (a practice still in effect). Lacking refrigeration, smoked meats served as replacements for the balance of the year. Sauerkraut with oil, for those who could afford it, made for a winter salad. Staple fare included corn bread, goat and/or sheep cheese, plus milk and yogurt. Summer brought fruits and some few other vegetables. Sugar, in limited supply, was reserved for coffee or tea (herbal); sweet desserts were special-occasion treats. It was a rare house without *šlivovica, loza,* or *vino* (wine). Given our view in the West of the dangers of a high salt and cholesterol diet, Montenegrins should have long since perished. Smothered in salt, slabs of heavily smoked bacon and other smoked meats and fish were fundamental to any Montenegrin kitchen and were consumed daily. When there was no meat, there was always animal fat, used extensively in cooking. Not that Montenegrins are big eaters, but what they did eat contained inordinate quantities of fat and salt.

So what precluded their succumbing to such a diet? One can only speculate. Perhaps hard, daily physical labor prevented the retention of fat leading to arteriosclerosis. Or could it have been deprivation? During wars, of which there were more than a few, food was infinitely more scarce and hunger prevalent. People went for years without bread, living on various *trave* (grasses)—*koprive* (nettles) in particular—made into soups, or prepared bread from ground corn husks. The choicest food, during war or otherwise, went to the men. Warriors required nourishment. Nor were the needs of children ignored, though many died young from illnesses related to poor nutrition and lack of proper medical attention. Women were at the end of the queue; what food remained after everyone was fed, not necessarily sated, was theirs.

With few available physicians—and those usually found in large cities—the practice of herbal medicine prevailed. Even final proclamation of death rested on the family or a villager with such expertise.

If the multiplicity of hard work, poverty, and deprivation contributes to longevity, there is no reason the women in this study should not be here. If stress resulting from perpetual wars, numerous deaths, and concerns over basic survival strengthens the will to live, then Montenegrin women are living proof. Suffering indeed may have intensified their resolve to endure, to sustain a culture demanding undue sacrifice. Allow for another consideration: pride in one's culture and identity.

It would be hard to find a woman prouder than a Montenegrin. She is pride incarnate. It would not be surprising to learn that the word was created specifically with her in mind. Here is a woman married to a man she did not know, bearing his many children under harrowing conditions, burying many of them in their early years. She would invariably lose husband, sons, and brothers through wars, starvation, and blood feuds (frequently burying them herself). Resigned to a life of incessant hardship, she accepted, without protest or inquiry, the fate bequeathed to her. With her every fiber she was committed to the preservation of the patriarchy into which she was born and the culture it had spawned, including her subservient status. Her pride emanated from the contribution she made to its continuity: raising children to uphold the legacy of their ancestors. In the main, that which nourishes her ego and sense of self is rooted in being the mother of warrior sons.

To see Montenegro as an unequivocally hermetic society is to err. The women in the North, separated by hundreds of kilometers of inhospitable terrain from the women in the South, know little of each other except that they reside in one country. Yet when comparing their life histories, one finds negligible difference. The tightly organized social system allows for no deviation from its prescribed order. What the uninitiated observe is a community of rigid conformity, devoid of individuality: see one, see them all, as it were. But that is pure delusion. The private persona behind the public persona is inaccessible to the outsider. Whatever occurs within the family and clan is carefully safeguarded. Beneath the seemingly homogeneous characteristics of the society at large lies a complex being, restrained from personal expression for the betterment of the collective. Somewhere within the confines of the family and clan, removed from public view, must exist a mechanism by which publicly repressed emotions can be privately articulated. If they could freely expound on their lives, what would they reveal, if anything? How is the sublimation of anger, jealousy, and hatred manifested? Has the art of self-control been cultivated to the point of inuring them to such emotions? Not likely. Then what is the secret? Unlocking that mystery is the challenge. One is privy to a cyclopean view of an exclusive society. Once trust has been firmly established, an outsider can penetrate this restricted world, but to what degree is debatable. Nonetheless, the doctrine by which they live and the face they present to the world can be corroborated by a glorious, admittedly brutal, history.

The purpose of my research is to open a window onto the original, fully tribal societies that are the foundations of our modern Western world. Anthropologists maintain that after we emerged from the caves, tribal cultures were the very first to exist. Warrior cultures were the most robust, and it is not surprising that one of them would persist somewhere, in some forgotten corner of the world, unvanquished.

Acknowledgments

Were it not for the assistance, guidance, and moral support of many on both sides of the Atlantic this book would have remained as it began—a "good idea"—rather than the book you now hold in your hands.

A posthumous thank you to Harvard Slavic scholar Albert Bates Lord for providing the initial encouragement and inspiration I needed to launch my "good idea." I was blessed in having received two awards facilitating my research: a sabbatical from Nassau Community College, for which I remain grateful to President Sean Fanelli and the Sabbatical Committee, and a State University of New York Scholar Award. Without the kind words of encouragement from Vice President Dr. Jack Ostling, Dr. William Atkins, the chair of the English Department, Professor Bruce Urquhart, and from my special friends and colleagues at NCC, there is no denying the "good idea" might easily have atrophied. Singular appreciation goes to the late Vera Jerwick and the professional staff of librarians at NCC and to librarian Tanya Gizdavčič at the New York Public Library's Slavic and Baltic Division, who tirelessly searched for and acquired material I requested from sources far and wide. In a computer emergency, real or imagined, I could always call on my friend and neighbor Miro Kresić: Thanks, Miro. I am eternally indebted to Vema Komich, my lifelong friend and "gal Friday." Thanks to Nina Dioguardi for her continual supply of magazine articles on diverse cultures and relevant topics.

Across the seas, a warm, heartfelt thank you to Dr. Branko Kostić, former president of Montenegro, for his invaluable counsel and material assistance and for engaging the noted Professor Vukale Djerković as an indispensable source of history and tradition. I salute Dr. Jovan P. Bojović, director of the History Institute in Podgorica (formerly Titograd), Montenegro, for sharing with me his fount of knowledge and making available the institute's rich collection of scholarship. *Puno hvala* to the many ethnologists, historians, and librarians at the institute who graciously offered and generously gave of their expertise and assistance.

Without the beneficence of 30 strangers who saw merit in my "good idea" by introducing me to the unique population of extraordinary women I bring to this study, I say, "Živeli." Through these remarkable women, whose words are indelibly etched on my memory, in whose beautiful creased faces were gathered the collected pain and pride of humanity, my life has been both enriched and humbled. A sincere and friendly *hvala* also to the chauffeurs assigned to transport me to my new, treasured friends.

I am forever thankful to Dušanka Jovićević and Nataša and Mihailo Mihailović for their incalculable aid in transcribing many of the original interviews. My sincere indebtedness is extended to Dr. Radojka Vukćević for providing me with supplemental research sources from afar throughout the writing of this book. A special hug for Dr. Dejan Jovičević, and Nenad Jovičević, and Lidija and Slobodan Djuranović, whose homes became a "receiving and forwarding station" for such material. My editors Don Ritchie and Mark Zadrozny never knew how much their patience and kind words were appreciated, even when—or especially when—the manuscript needed revision and when I "overshot" certain deadlines. And what would writers do without text editors? India Koopman is *my* savior. Their place in editors' heaven is firmly secure. Mary and Philip Hart, publishers and editors of *Serb World U.S.A.,* more than deserve a warm handshake for their generous offer of maps and photographs, some appearing in this book.

To my husband, Wallace, and son, Mark, nonprofessional in-house editors, special hugs for the interminable time spent reading and rereading each revision without ever a complaint or sigh, and for their broad knowledge of the history of Montenegro. I cannot give more than a mother's love to Mark for spending incalculable hours at my side, making suggestions and recalling certain anecdotes and unique experiences during his videotaping of this project, while I plunked at the word processor. To my dearest daughter, Andrea, I owe my love and at least a manicure to compensate the endless hours spent entering my translated transcriptions into the computer.

My father—who sacrificed his life for his family—remains the bedrock of my life. The stories, myths, and legends of *stari kraj* (the old country) my mother told me were those my narrators heard from their mothers and told to their children and that I eventually shared with my own children, thus bringing them full circle. My mother instilled in me a sense of the significance of the past and the importance of family and tradition, telling me I made her proud in writing this book. To my natal family, my brothers and sisters— those with whom I lovingly shared the first two decades of my life—I say, "Perhaps this book will assist in providing a cathartic understanding of who and why we are." I must apologize to my husband and children for my intermittent curtness and impatience, although, *God knows,* I tried to be positive. You brought love where there was exasperation, tranquility where there was anxiety, a smile where there was a frown, energy where there was lethargy, faith where there was despair. For that and much more, I embrace you all.

I did not write this book without some degree of angst. My primary motive was to introduce through personal narratives an undocumented population of tribal European women born in the nineteenth century. The interviews speak for themselves. Placing these women's lives in historical perspective by anchoring them in a society about which equally little is known was a further imperative. My third and most agonizing task was to remain objective. Without sentimentality and hyperbole, I was obligated to present their world with the honesty it deserves. To that end, if I have failed it is solely because of my own limitations.

Introduction

In the 1960s I spent two full years living in Gornja Moraca, the home of a mountain tribe in the Brda district of Montenegro. It took five hours on foot to reach this isolated, traditional tribe, so it is safe to say that I—like Zorka Milich—went to Montenegro in search of its past.

As an anthropologist fascinated by Montenegrin culture, I will never forget the first time I heard the loud report of dynamite echoing up and down that remote valley and, with a trace of alarm, asked what was happening. "Oh, nothing out of the way," answered my favorite informant, Milena Lukovac, who then added, "some woman has just borne a son."

As a novice field-worker I had read about joyous gunfire in historical times, for Montenegrins always discharged firearms at festive meetings of the tribes and at weddings. They still do today. But this was my first exposure to the birth of a boy punctuated by gunfire, and I knew from my reading that a baby girl would have warranted no such salute. In Montenegro, the difference in life experience that comes from being born male or female is far greater than it is in most other countries.

In 1965 Milena Lukovac, a woman of the Upper Moraca Tribe without any formal schooling, was 77 years old. She died a few years later. In 1995 she would have been the same age as the women whose words are immortalized in this book, about 100. My conversation with Milena brought to mind something I had read in a history book, a saying once used to commemorate the birth of a daughter in Crmnička Nahija, a tribal district in Old Montenegro, down by the seacoast. On the birth of a girl the people of one tribe there were known to say, "A snake has been born in our house." I mentioned this to Milena, and she affirmed that people don't like it when they get daughters. "You lavish loving care on a daughter," she said, "and then she marries into another clan to provide them with sons and a willing worker."

One might well wonder what it was like to be a woman in a society so openly biased against females. Zorka Milich, through an imaginative field-work project, has provided the answer. A woman's happiness in traditional

Montenegro was determined by repeated throws of the genetic dice. If blessed with many sons, she was widely respected and appreciated by her husband's family and clan. If she bore just a single grown son things were rather dicey, for the average traditional Montenegrin family lost many of its men to warfare, feuding, or raiding. If she had only daughters, her value was much diminished and her life seen as little more fulfilled than that of the pitiful woman with no children at all.

Because the warlike Christian Serbs of Montenegro were a thorn in the side of the mighty Ottoman Empire for several centuries, many foreigners visited them in the 1800s for political reasons or out of sheer curiosity about these crusading Christian warriors. This procession included the British writer Charles Lamb and his wife Mary. For several centuries until the 1850s these formidable Serbs existed as "Europeans" who lived in free and independent tribes, an enclave of free and equal Christians who were all but encircled by the Ottoman Empire. In 1850 they began to form the tiny Kingdom of Montenegro, which survived until 1916.

The women whose words Zorka Milich preserves in this book grew up in a unique tribal kingdom that attacked the Ottoman Empire in 1875, taking over much of Hercegovina, and then attacked Turkish Albania in 1912. This started the First Balkan War, which led directly to the assassination of Archduke Ferdinand in Sarajevo in 1914. Suffice it to say that the 20 some odd Montenegrin tribes have played a sizable role in Balkan and world history, and the women are fully as proud of this heritage as the men.

Early reports about the tribal period came from Austrian, British, and French spies and historians, and these reports invariably concentrate on the males as illiterate warriors quite sophisticated in the ways of politics. The extreme submission of females to males is noted in passing, as is the women's sometimes active support in warfare and feuding. It is the role of the male warrior that is extremely well known, however, whereas only a bare outline of women's lives is available. There does exist in the Serbian language a book called *Outstanding Female Montenegrins*, but it has never been translated and in any event the case histories involved women who were atypical. They all stepped squarely into the male role to perform as heroes.

In the tribe of Gornja Moraca there is a local epic that was still being sung frequently in the 1960s by *guslars*, men who improvise heroic epics in the traditional manner. It tells of how the Turks came in force to plunder the tribe in 1820, grabbed a young mother, Plana Dragović, and threw her suckling baby into the river. Plana jeered at the men of the tribe, who were hiding in the forest, and then she grabbed the pistol of the Turkish leader who was abducting her and killed him. Shamed, the men of Morača then fell on the Islamic enemy and dealt them a decisive defeat.

Such tales of women who stepped over the line are fascinating, but they tell us little about the ordinary life of traditional Montenegrin women. Here the work of Mary Edith Durham is helpful. Durham was a British nurse who traveled to the South Balkans at the turn of the twentieth century and became an expert on Montenegrin and Albanian tribal customs. She took special interest in the female sphere, and her work provides a salutary augmentation to Montenegrin ethnography. Her accounts deal with the time period when most of the old women interviewed in this book were brides. Her best accounts are found in *Some Tribal Origins*, published in 1928; they make for useful background reading.

A Stranger's Supper provides the rich materials needed to really understand the traditional concerns of women in Montenegro. Zorka Milich lets her amazing centenarians speak for themselves, with minimal editing and only such amplification as is necessary. In reading these interviews, one must keep in mind the context in which they were conducted. First, the interviewer is not only another woman but a woman who speaks the local Serbian dialect and is of Montenegrin descent. This enables her informants to speak from their hearts. Second, there is the matter of cultural context. There exists a peculiarly Montenegrin style of telling about one's life experiences, one that is more pronounced in women than in men. Most older Montenegrins have experienced dire hardship of one kind or another, and the cultural style of autobiographical discourse reflects this strongly.

After four centuries of frequent warfare, raiding, and feuding, the vocabulary of suffering, sorrow, and hardship is rich and well developed. Montenegrins—the women in particular—are prone to dwell on such negatives when sharing their experiences, and they readily turned to the language of hyperbole in speaking with Zorka Milich. Montenegrins also wax poetic when they speak of valor or of sons. Heroism, continuation of the male line, and suffering are important themes in traditional Montenegrin culture.

Like illiterate people everywhere, Montenegrin women of this generation lost many of their children to enteritis or other diseases, and they lost many of their men to warfare. The generation of the women interviewed here lived through several Balkan Wars, the Great War in Europe, and World War II, which in Yugoslavia also involved a bloody civil conflict. Earlier, Montenegrins fought for centuries to live free of Ottoman control, and sometimes they endured truly genocidal attacks in which the men were hunted down like rabbits and the women and children were led off in chains to Turkish slave markets. The result was a warrior ethos and a society in which males were inordinately valued not only as fighters who strengthened the tribe but as symbols of clan continuity.

Most of the women in this book were born as Eastern Orthodox Serbs, but the modern Republic of Montenegro also includes Serbs and Albanians who long ago turned to Islam and also some Albanians who are Catholic. The interviews follow the mix of religions in the composition of modern Montenegro: most of the women are Christian Serbs, while other ethnicities are sampled. It is clear that in many ways the people in this region shared a single basic culture that focused on women producing sons. These sons became warriors who fought to defend their tribe, went out raiding to plunder their enemies, and feuded at home as well, because honorable tribal warriors everywhere engage in feuding.

In a sense, the Albanian interviews present a clearer view of the tribal past than do the interviews with Orthodox Serbs, for the Montenegrin Serbs have lived as a nation rather than as a collection of independent tribes for nearly a century and a half. National governments do not like raiding because it makes for trouble between nations, and they do not like feuding because they insist on law and order. The Albanians in the north of Albania and Montenegro still engage in feuds, and a Catholic Albanian woman tells about losing a son to them.

Although feuding has been long suppressed among traditional Montenegrin Serbs, its effects on the lives of women linger. When feuds were endemic among the tribes, women had to do most of the heavy work out of doors because as females they were exempt from all the revenge killing. By contrast, the men were either in hiding or engaged in hunting down their enemies. More generally, Montenegrin sex roles were forged in a perpetual "wartime" economy. These tribesmen fought frequently against local Ottoman lords, and because of overpopulation they had to go out raiding for six months every year. This left most of the subsistence work to women. Serbs in Belgrade joke about Montenegrins, and the jokes run in two directions. One is that the women have a very low status, and the other is that the men are almost unbelievably lazy.

When I was in Montenegro in the mid-1960s I had a chance to check out these stereotypes in the field, and I found Montenegrin men to be extremely hardworking except in the wintertime. When days are long, they may work steadily for 12 hours or more, and heavier work, like cutting hay, is left to them. Women's outdoor work is also hard, for Montenegro has always been land poor and labor intensive. When winter comes the gardens are under snow and the men merely feed their livestock and chop wood, whereas the women still have total responsibility for child care and household duties.

In the tribe of Upper Morača, one of the women's greatest burdens was carrying water. It was shameful for a man to do this, even though there was only one spring in the scattered settlement and the paths were strewn with rocks. The barrels of water women carried on their backs were extremely heavy; the only woman in the village allowed to use the family horse to carry this burden was a cripple. In short, there is some truth to the jokes one hears.

The most visible form of oral tradition in Montenegro is the heroic epic, which only men are allowed to sing unless exceptional circumstances exist. (I recorded one case in the Kuči Tribe of a father teaching his daughter to sing epics as a cure for fear of lightning.) This Homeric culture had its bards, but every individual Montenegrin also has a personal oral tradition, the story of his or her life. Like the heroic epics, these autobiographical tales harken to certain themes and involve the use of a distinctive poetic language.

I have mentioned that personal autobiographies in Montenegro focus on hardships, difficulties, the crosses people have borne. The descriptive language is rich, and it is decidedly richer when employed by women. While talking in this vein, an old woman is likely to call you *bolan* (painful one) or *jadan* (sorrowful one) and to speak of *teskoce* (hardships) or in terms of a *teret* (a burden) or of *jade* (which also means hardships). Although such expression is given to hyperbole, I do not mean to say that life in Montenegro 80 years ago was easy or that it was not more difficult for women than for men. Traditional Montenegrin women were dealt a large share of hardship, and they feel free to speak about this.

The life of a Montenegrin woman as I saw it three decades ago in the most isolated tribe in Montenegro was never easy. Still, much depended on the makeup of the household. A house with several women made possible the sharing of work, and if these women had sons they eventually had daughters-in-law to work for them. An unlucky woman would be barren and have many older adults to take care of, relatives of her husband.

One thing I noted early in my fieldwork was what the life of a married woman did to her appearance. By the time she was 30, a woman with a large family to work for appeared to be old beyond her years and yet ageless, and tired. By contrast, women who never married or who married but failed to bear children appeared to age gracefully. Such women had other crosses to bear. If they failed to marry, it was for one of two reasons. Either they were *kurvas*, a derogatory term used by one of the women in the interviews, which means "slut," or they were ugly, which to a Montenegrin usually means being of very short stature. In either case, they were considered old maids. The word for this in village Montenegro means "a person who is left sitting," and there is no such term for men.

For a married woman, the worst burden was if she failed to produce sons. She had an ever-expectant husband waiting for that precious cargo, and her entire self-esteem was caught up in this basic female mission in life: to bear sons and to be the foundation of the household in which a family is raised, one that keeps the male line going. She was completely dependent on the luck of the draw. If she had 10 daughters to care for, her husband would still want to have a son. If she had two or three sons, he might want several more just for "insurance." Death took away many Montenegrin sons and daughters, and the sons were sorely missed.

If sons involved duty and self-fulfillment, the emotionally richest relationship for a traditional female was that of a sister with her brother. Sisters doted on their brothers, and even today they seldom ask for a legal share of the patriarchal property when the father dies. Brothers were left behind on their sister's marriage, but she elevated them almost to sainthood and counted on them as distant protectors. Leaving individual personalities aside, a woman suffered much more from the loss of a brother or a son than from the loss of a husband or a daughter. It was her sons, of course, who would look after her in old age.

There was a definite progression through a typical married woman's life cycle. At birth she was resented genealogically and economically because she was not a male. As a young girl, in spite of the love that arose spontaneously in the family, she bore two burdens. One was knowing that she would never contribute heirs to her own clan. The other was the knowledge that she was felt to be a poor economic investment. Her natal family would nurture her and teach her to work, but her husband's family would reap the benefits. Milena Lukovac once told me rather philosophically that the ideal arrangement would be to marry your own daughters to your sons—but that would be incest.

As a bride, a young woman had to be totally *skromna* (modest) and *stidna* (bashful). At the wedding she could meet no one's eyes, and as a young wife she could neither smoke nor curse with the choice words reserved for men. She was an outsider living in a close-knit family of males, and she was there to prove herself by bearing sons, working hard, and avoiding any sexual impropriety. This last included not only committing adultery but leaning "suggestively" as she sat in a chair or showing even a hint of her knees when men were present. Gradually, however, things changed for the typical married woman.

By the age of 50 she was beginning to use male swear words, to smoke tobacco instead of circumspectly sniffing snuff, and to drink freely in company. Her life was far more free, and she could and usually did engage in the earthy sexual joking that Montenegrins are so fond of. Whether she bore an ample number of sons or not, she gradually became a member of her *dom*, her husband's household, and in effect became respected as an honorary clan member. If she bore the household and clan sons, her status and self-esteem were all the stronger. The women presented here had all reached this stage of freedom; indeed, they had lived "as free as men" for nearly half a century. As older women they were able to speak with self-assurance and little inhibition. This shines forth in the interviews.

Traditional Montenegrins are a most interesting breed of people, and, if anything, the women are more interesting than the men because they had to cope with leaving the clan of their birth. If she has no sons, a woman is often blamed. This can become ugly, for women without children are almost automatically suspected of being witches. A Montenegrin witch does not ride a broomstick; rather, she magically "eats the souls" of the children in her extended family. Her motive is jealousy, and her mode of locomotion is winged; she can assume the form of a moth or a bird and enter a house to kill her relatives' children. One of my neighbors in Upper Morača hadn't spoken to his childless sister for years because of such beliefs. No such stigma attaches itself to men who fail to marry or produce children.

In America there is a great deal of taking sides by the sexes, and these days gender roles tend to be defined quite differently by most males and females. I spent three years altogether in Montenegro, and what struck me was that women seemed quickest to judge other women as being of little account. Women complained about their personal lots, but they didn't really seem to question the overall system.

Having said this, I should also say that there is still enormous respect in Montenegro today for a "good woman," one who is virtuous and hardworking and with some luck bears lots of sons, just as there was in the 1960s when I lived there and just as there was back in 1900 or in the tribal period. For all the deprecation of women, there is a relatively little-voiced but deeply felt appreciation of them as the foundation of the family. Because continuation of the patrilineal family is everything in Montenegro, women are highly valued. A woman who bears sons at least has a chance at happiness, but disease, warfare, and feuding cut down many a son in the early 1900s, when the women interviewed here were young. Their stories may be expressed vehemently and with poetic pronouncements of pain and sorrow, but they are far from being exaggerated in any serious way. Their cultural tradition was one built on several centuries of constant warfare and loss of sons, and warfare and loss of sons also afflicted the next generation of women after them because of World War II.

I originally went to study Montenegro to see what four centuries of intensive, violent conflict can do to a people, and the oral histories printed here say all too clearly what they did to women. Every word spoken by these women rings true to me as one who knew dozens of older women 30 years ago, women who would be about 100 years old today. Zorka Milich is to be commended for having carried forward this imaginative and unusual project in anthropology, for the words of her informants immortalize the thoughts and feelings of their supposedly weaker sex, which has been heard from too seldom and too little.

CHRISTOPHER BOEHM
Director, Jane Goodall Research Center
University of Southern California

A house does not rest on the ground;
it rests on a woman

MONTENEGRO: THE WOMEN BEHIND THE WARRIORS

O smallest among peoples! rough-rock-throne
Of Freedom! Warriors beating back the swarm
Of Turkish Islam for five hundred years,
Great Tzernagora! never since thine own
Black ridges drew the cloud and brake the storm
Has breathed a race of mightier mountaineers.
—Alfred Lord Tennyson, "Montenegro"

A brief understanding of the history and social structure of Montenegro, a hauntingly beautiful and eerily seductive land, "a soil barren of everything but men" (Djilas, 130), is critical in anchoring the lives of the women in this study. A literal terra firma and a relative terra incognita, this soil is perhaps less fertile, mile for mile, than that of any other region in Europe. Despite this fact—or perhaps because of it—the area has been famous for millennia as the home of fierce warriors and inconceivable hardship—the proverbial no-man's-land. Its present population is slightly more than 500,000, a mix of Serbs, Slavic Muslims, and Albanians (Muslim and Roman Catholic), with Serbian Eastern Orthodox Christians being in the majority.

The area has been habitable only by those hardy souls capable of tolerating—indeed thriving amid—its barren limestone crags and mountains and its indomitable and intolerant warrior tribesmen, the first of whom were the warlike and legendarily hostile Illyrian tribes of antiquity. The Celts, arriving in 300 B.C., were the first to accomplish this feat, leaving "a deep mark on the people of to-day by the infusion of Celtic blood" (Durham 1971, 2). The nations and empires surrounding what became Montenegro preferred to adopt an "avoid, not confront" policy. The Illyrians were finally subjugated in A.D. 9 by the Roman emperor Tiberius. After having withstood warfare with the Macedonian and Roman empires for hundreds of years, Illyrian tribesmen were ultimately incorporated into the front rank of the Roman legions. Notable sons of Illyrian peasants even rose to the ranks of Roman

1

emperors: Claudius, Diocletian, Aurelian, Valerian, Maximian, and Constantine the Great (Kuzmanović, 17–19). The arrival of Slavs in the early seventh century, during the reign of the Byzantine emperor Heraclius (610–41), marked the beginning of what is now known as the Montenegrin people (Pavlovich, 6).

Montenegro, a Venetian Italian word and a literal translation of Crna Gora (Black Mountain), was at one time considerably smaller than at present. It was only in 1796 that it annexed the Brda region, northeast of old Montenegro. Following the expulsion of the Turks in Grahovo in 1858, the surrounding territory and the Savnik region came under Montenegrin control (Treadway, 7). The greatest territorial gains came through the Congress of Berlin in 1878, substantially expanding the territory on three sides, including the port city of Bar on the Adriatic Sea. It was not until sometime later that the land necessary to reach the sea was acquired, creating an entrée to the outside world. Two years after obtaining Bar, the small port of Ulcinj on the Adriatic was secured. The country had now grown to twice its original size (Ražnatović, 80–84).

During the Balkan Wars of 1912–13, thousands of Montenegrin men who had earlier immigrated to America returned to defend their homeland, determined to keep it free of foreign domination. Numbered among this group were my paternal grandfather, Boško Mašanović—later anglicized to Masanovich—and his two sons, my father, Jovan, and his brother, Vido. As soldiers in a ragtag army, with little or no training, they fought around Skadar, Albania. Starvation was pervasive. Being hungry for days and in search of food, my father and uncle entered a poor one-room Albanian house, where they found a terrified young mother with several emaciated children. Desperately rummaging through the room and finding nothing, my father suddenly spied a trunk. Confident the food was there, he opened it. But he was unprepared for what he uncovered, a sight that haunted him for he rest of his life.

In the trunk lay the dead body of a small child. "Hunger," said my father, "has neither eyes nor conscience, especially to an exhausted and starving young soldier." As he was about to lift up the child to get to where he thought the bread was hidden, his brother shouted, "If you know God at all, close the trunk and let's get out of here!" Startled into confronting his inhumanity, an aspect of himself that glaringly surfaced now that he was face to face with his own mortality, he fled the house. The mother and her starving brood were shadows of himself, his brother, and the mother and family they had left behind. Somewhere this woman's husband, too, must be foraging for food, attempting to stave off his own death.

These thoughts plagued my father. Both he and his brother were certain the mother purposely kept the dead child in the trunk to safeguard food, trusting no one would suspect it was there. By not burying her child, she protected her other children from starvation. My father used to say, "No human being is as sacrificing as a mother, be she Albanian, Montenegrin, or from some other place."

After the Balkan Wars and World War I, my grandfather chose to remain in his native land; his two sons returned to America. The Statue of Liberty may have welcomed back these two immigrants, who returned to American shores *trbuhom za kruhom* (stomach in search of bread), but many Americans, whose parents themselves had been immigrants, did not. In the early 1920s, my father and uncle were living and working in West Virginia. One day, standing in line to pick up their mail at the local post office, they encountered the prejudice unknown in their native land. When the postal clerk asked my father his name so that he could be given his mail, he answered, "Masanovich." "What?" said the clerk. My father repeated his name, and the clerk repeated his question. From the line came a voice, "Didn't you hear him? He said, 'Masonofabitch.' " My proud Montenegrin father, his brother following closely, took after the man. Both brothers, well over six feet tall (average height for Montenegrins), caught up with him in the middle of a bridge. My father lifted the man over his shoulders and was about to toss him into the water, when his brother cried out, "If you know God, put the man down, and let's get out of here before they catch us and kill us." Perceiving their imminent death as a real possibility, they left town that instant. Their experience was hardly unique. My father-in-law, himself a Montenegrin, and many others endured similar ordeals.

A number of years later, my father went back to Montenegro for a wife, his family having found him a bride. Shortly thereafter, he and his 17-year-old bride, my mother, boarded a ship and disembarked at Ellis Island. There, frightened and intimidated, his *nevjesta* (bride) was hospitalized with pneumonia for 10 days. Thirteen years and seven children later, she became a widow in a strange land, among strange people.

Like any young Montenegrin woman who leaves behind her natal village to marry a stranger in an alien village, my mother relinquished a familiar environment. But she had also crossed an ocean to live in a culture demanding assimilation, among people whose language she neither spoke nor understood. Onerous as the existence of a woman living in Montenegro was, she at least suffered in a land where the traditions and language were familiar and where she was respected. She did not experience life as a "greenhorn" immigrant, as did her sister in the New World. Young, widowed Jovanka, separated by thousands of miles from family and what she knew best, struggled alone, with seven small children clinging to her for their existence and survival. Today, in her mid-80s, she often remarks, "We made it through."

The return from America of my father, grandfather, uncle, and many other Montenegrins to their native land *da brane otadjbinu* (to defend their fatherland) during the Balkan Wars was not in vain. Despite the territory gained at the Congress of Berlin in 1878, serious problems between the "Turks" (Slavic Muslims) and Montenegrins had persisted. Without government funding, Montenegrins living on the border were responsible for guarding it against pervasive theft. These border skirmishes culminated in the Balkan Wars (Rakočević, 485). The land gained in the 1912–13 wars (Treadway, 3)—the Sandžak area in the northeast, divided between Montenegro and Serbia in 1912, and the western region of Kosovo (203)—was substantial, increasing the Muslim population as well. The Muslims of the Sandžak are local Slavs who had converted to Islam, unlike those in the Kosovo region, who are Albanians. The inhabitants of Malëesia (northern Albania) are primarily Roman Catholic. A small portion of Malëesia's eastern border, Tuzi and the area south of Lake Scutari, also came under Montenegrin rule (3). With these annexations, Montenegro reached its maximum size. This tiny, inconspicuous, impoverished land prevailed for centuries as an unremitting thorn in the sides of two powerful empires: Ottoman and Austro-Hungarian, oppressors of the surrounding area for more than 500 years.

Montenegro began as a Slavic state, part of Stefan Dušan's great Serb empire during the Middle Ages, until its collapse in the fourteenth century, when it gained its independence. Predating present-day Montenegro, Zeta, a relatively fertile lowland, extending from northern Albania and along the Adriatic Coast, fought to remain independent (5). Scutari, then the capital and the major city in present-day Albania, situated on Lake Scutari, lies on the periphery of Montenegro's border. Today both Montenegro and Albania share the lake—ever a source of contention. The Battle of Kosovo in 1389 signaled the death knell for the independence of the Balkan peninsula, fusing it with the Turkish Empire. Scutari was a Venetian city between 1396 and 1405, when it was recaptured by the Ottomans. To preclude being consumed by the Ottomans, who had confiscated Zeta's lowlands, Ivan Crnojević, Zeta's ruler, moved his capital to Cetinje, where it would remain until the end of World War II. (At the end of the war, Tito relocated the capital to Podgorica, a commercial town in Zeta, renaming it Titograd.) Crnojević's rule weakened, and Montenegro became a Turkish province during the latter part of the fifteenth century and the early sixteenth century, with Crnojević's son as ruler. Following his short-lived reign from 1514 to 1528, Montenegro reclaimed its land and independence from the Turks (6).

Freedom-loving Montenegrins did not organize a state in the real sense of the word; rather, patriarchal power rested with clan chieftains. But final decisions were made by the people, through council and assembly meetings. When they realized that more cohesiveness was necessary than the tribal and clan system could accommodate, they decided on a unique form of government. To avoid infringement on the sovereignty of the tribe, they opted against a secular type of government in favor of vesting authority in Orthodox bishops, or *vladike*. The new rulers of Montenegro were elected prince-bishops (*vladike*), empowered with complete temporal and ecclesiastic control. Their role was not to enforce their authority but to mediate and act as the conscience of the people (Petrovich, xix–xx). With the election of Bishop Danilo I in 1696, the Petrović family ruled until World War I, when its first king, Nikola I, a significant player in the European political arena, was exiled in 1916.

Because Orthodox bishops were celibate (Orthodox parish priests were required to marry), the office passed from uncle to nephew or grandnephew until 1852, when Prince Danilo I, the lawgiver, secularized Montenegro (Treadway, 6). On the whole, though the prince introduced a formal legal system, it coexisted with tribal laws. Unless transgressions were so egregious that they could be adjudicated only by the courts, tribal law was exercised.

Such practices underwent some changes at the end of World War II. In 1946, a new form of government was implemented—a socialist system with a new legal policy. It, too, was not wholly successful. Modern Montenegro remains relatively provincial in its makeup; it is a composite of large rural areas, small to intermediate towns, and one large city—the capital, Podgorica. As a result, tribal customs and traditions prevail throughout the land. Extended families are as vital and as cohesive today as they were in the "traditional" period—which began with the formation of Montenegro in the tenth century—practicing the same or similar beliefs as did their ancestors.

Ubiquitous campaigns by the Turks notwithstanding, Montenegrins resolutely struggled to maintain their independence, frequently at awesome sacrifice. In a "handful of illiterate mountaineers," writes one noted historian, "was vested an importance and even greatness that far transcended its numbers and conditions . . . a perpetually embattled warrior race" became "the symbol of freedom in the Turkish-dominated Balkans" (Petrovich, xx). They are "Christendom's most extraordinary people," states William Ewart Gladstone, nineteenth-century British statesman and Homeric scholar, whose "traditions . . . exceed in glory those of Marathon and Thermopylae and all the war traditions of the world" (Jovanovich, x). This is not to imply that Montenegrins had an obsession with death, although they have had their share of it. Nor were they hardened to it. It is that they so valued freedom that they were willing to die for it. It was every Montenegrin's wish that he not die in bed. Dying in defense of one's land and honor was a warrior's aspiration.

Montenegrins lamented the loss of their brethren to Islam. The most celebrated epic poem in Serbo-Croatian literature, *Gorski Vjenac*, or *The Mountain Wreath*, composed by Montenegro's revered bishop-prince, Vladika Peter II Njegoš (1813–51), chronicles the flight of Christians from occupied Turkish lands into Montenegro:

> Mighty lions have become meek peasants. Rash and greedy converted to Islam. . . . Those who escaped before the Turkish sword, those who did not

blaspheme at the True Faith, those who refused to be thrown into chains, took refuge here in these lofty mountains to shed their blood together and to die, heroically to keep the sacred oath, their lovely name, and their holy freedom (lines 259–68). . . . I would like to invite the leaders of the converts to a meeting of all of our brothers, we'll guarantee their lives until they leave. Perhaps they will return then to our faith and extinguish the flame of our blood-feud (lines 677–82). . . . It may not be the turncoats' fault as much. The infidel seduced them with falsehood and entangled them in the devil's nets. But what is man? In truth, a weak creature! (lines 760–63) . . . We put under our sharp sabers all those who did not want to be baptized by us . . . but all those who bowed . . . and crossed themselves . . . we accepted and hailed as our brothers (lines 2599–603).

According to legend, on Christmas Eve in 1702, Montenegrins killed every Turk and Slavic convert to Islam on their soil, but not before offering every convert the opportunity to forsake Islam. "When morning dawned not a Mussulman remained alive on the soil of Montenegro" (Denton, 231). This legend has become every Montenegrin's truth. "Montenegro . . . reeks of heroism," writes Rebecca West (1010), justifying this event: "A man is not a man if he will not save his seed" (1008). They are "Homeric heroes: . . . brave, and beautiful, and vainglorious" (1009). With consecrated maces, so the legend goes, the five Martinović brothers responsible for the massacre "may be assumed to have been of flawless and inhuman beauty, like the Montenegrins of today" (1008). For the people, *The Mountain Wreath* "contained higher truths, their truths," unveiling "something untransitory, something that would last as long as their race and tongue survived . . . expressed in the language of everyday" (Djilas, 130). For people scarcely familiar with the Bible, it "might have served as such a book" (130). So beloved is *The Mountain Wreath* that to this day Montenegrins proudly commit it to memory—male and female, young and old, literate and illiterate—including the women whose memories inform this book.

Consistent with all traditional patriarchies, Montenegro, "a refuge-area warrior society" (Boehm, 39), had little tolerance for change despite wars of occupation: males were to dominate; females were marginalized. The patriarchy notwithstanding, Montenegro demanded of both sexes strict adherence to centuries-old values: all were mandated to respect, to nurture, and to glorify their warrior history, handed down through an intricately developed oral epic tradition, including lengthy poems sung to the accompaniment of the *gusle* (an ancient one-stringed instrument). Epic poems "glorified the heroes of the nation's past," depicting "the struggles of the nation against outside forces" (Lord, 7). Such poetry, venerating national heroes, provided the moral and spiritual sustenance crucial for survival in a harsh, isolated land. The Montenegrin reverence for language and exultation in a proud though violent past have produced many writers, documenting in prose and verse battles and warriors of old defending a society resolved in its determination to be free.

The age of enlightenment—that is, the desire for knowledge—developed in Montenegro long before the emergence of a national Serbian literature; it can be traced to a hagiography of St. Vladimir in the eleventh century or the first half of the twelfth (Stanojević, xiii). In the thirteenth century, immediately prior to the collapse of independent Serbian lands, on the request of the priests from the archdiocese of the Diocletian church and town youths—whose favorite pastime was listening to and reading about war— Father Dukljan wrote a chronicle in Latin (xiii–iv). The world's second movable-type printing press was developed in Cetinje, Montenegro, in the Middle Ages, 40 or 50 years after the invention of the Gutenberg press in Germany (xv).

Nevertheless, illiteracy prevailed in Montenegro well into the twentieth century. Listening to the centenarian women interviewed here, however, one would never know it. These illiterate tribal women speak of history as if they had read it in books, relating the story of the 1389 Battle of Kosovo as if it were a current event (Nenadović, 73). It was slightly more than a century ago, with the help of foreign aid, that penurious Montenegro began extending an education to a limited number of females. On a visit to the czar in St. Petersburg (1868), Prince Nikola scored a coup for the women in his land. As a sign of the deep affection held by the Russian czar for his Slavic Christian Orthodox brothers in Montenegro, he provided financial support for the creation and maintenance of a school for girls in Cetinje, in honor of his czarina, Empress Maria (Dragović, 3). This impoverished land, perpetually at war, welcomed "twelve delicate Montenegrin girls" to its "*Ženski zavod*" (Women's Institute) in 1869 (Dragićević, 131), where they were instructed in reading, writing, and handicrafts (134).

Deeply ingrained in the collective psyche of patriarchal Montenegro is a sense of historicism unique in Europe: "The tribesmen still feel strongly the presence of their tribal social life and tribal identity" (Boehm, 3). The traditional tribes were extremely rigid and stable organizations, led by the most respected and heroic men to defend against other tribes and Turks, who often confiscated their pastures or abducted their women. For these reasons men were always armed, prepared for battle to safeguard their painfully earned rights (Vujačić, 53–54). Within tribes, each male member was considered equal, except where there were weak, indigent, and less respected men, in which case strong tribal chiefs enjoyed significantly more rights (61).

What bolstered Montenegro's persistent battle for autonomy was a code of values celebrating honor and heroism—*čojstvo i junaštvo* (Miljanov, 107). To maintain this code, powerful clans married from similar clans. People believed that such societies would produce genetically superior warriors. Three basic components, evident in the anthropological characteristics of the

Dinaric race—inhabitants of the southeastern range of the Alps, extending along the Adriatic coast of the former Yugoslavia into northern Albania— have informed the "creed" of Montenegrins and those from Hercegovina:

1. The intrusion of other races has a negative impact on the uniformity and harmony of a people.
2. Short stature, physical unattractiveness, obesity, physical defects, limited intelligence, and indolence are persuasive warnings against miscegenation.
3. The absolute value of greatness is embodied in a "good home," in a woman from good *soja* (lineage) whose grandchildren will then be either heroes or wise and melancholy (Gezeman, 146–48).

Montenegrins believed that such a carefully conceived population creates essential spiritual and moral elements critical in social and family relationships, in the containment and/or resolutions of conflicts, and in the understanding of relations between friend and foe, thus engendering a harmonious collective sensibility in whose midst religion plays an important role, though not in the traditional sense (Vujačić, 63).

Montenegrins have been Eastern Orthodox Christians for just short of a millennium, practicing an Orthodoxy adapted to tribal laws and beliefs, a form of "religious mysticism" (100–101). Subsequently, and quite naturally, this Orthodoxy fused with societal moral ethics and the two became an organic whole. Parents taught their children to believe in a higher power about which they themselves knew little. By upholding all Christian tenets and their patron saints, they learned how to defend the holy days of family, clan, and tribe. To sacrifice one's life for another was fortuitous for the deceased. Heroic death had inordinate moral significance.

Christianity affected males specifically, notably clerics, who were not exempt from battle. Because they had frequently engaged in murder during their lifetime, clerics were forbidden the Orthodox confessional (Boehm, 47). *Pops* (illiterate priests appointed by the tribes), *vladikas,* and *kaludjers* (monks) "went to war like anyone else" (47). *Kaludjers* and *vladikas* remained celibate; *pops* were permitted one marriage (47). The clergy, including the bishop as ranking official in the land, did not have an easy time in tribal Montenegro.

Reconciling church law with tribal behavior, such as blood feuds, was a formidable task. Among the tribesmen, feuds routinely took precedence over appeasement, despite the *vladika*'s threat of damnation. Threats of excommunication meant little in a society only loosely religious. Understanding his people was his strength. When appropriate, he cunningly invoked their maniacal preoccupation with male progeny. Failing with other tactics, he resorted to a curse: "May the black flag hang from the ridge pole of your house!" Without sons, that house would be forever extinguished. The very idea of such a life forced Montenegrins to take notice (68–69). For others, hubris more often than not overrode any threats from a higher power, compelling them to continue with what they knew best: feuding. Montenegrins lived in a perpetual state of war or preparedness for war against the ever-threatening Turks. Among themselves, they had to contend with continual intertribal conflicts, often leading to blood vendettas.

*　*　*

Blood revenge, a form of "conflict management" (87), was a basic factor in the "moral system and its operation" among Montenegrins, "a people who were extremely sensitive in the matter of honor" (85). Maintaining one's own reputation and that of the clan, in which each man was considered a brother, was moral justification for the retribution of blood. The most common cause for homicidal conflicts centered on sexual morality, specifically, attacks on a woman's honor. A husband safeguarded and defended his wife's honor no less than did her father and brother before she was married (Baković, 148). I heard of just such an account.

In the 1920s, the wife and mother of three children in a respected family was in danger of being seduced by the village womanizer. To preclude dishonor, her husband repeatedly warned the miscreant to desist from this behavior, but to no avail. Desperate, he solicited intervention by the family of the scoundrel, which proved ineffective. At his wit's end, he waylaid and killed the rogue on a deserted road. Secure in the knowledge that he had done what was honorable, he informed the family of the deceased about what had transpired, even pointing out the location of the body. The family supported his actions, shook his hand, and buried their son. Both families were relieved of the potential disgrace and the specter of a blood vendetta. So ingrained was this convention that during the reign of Peter I (1903–21), 82 men lost their lives within 16 years over the insult of one woman (Gezeman, 168). In the 1930s, eight men lost their lives in a blood feud over a woman (Baković, 148).

It was perfectly acceptable for a female to participate in blood feuds. Since killing a woman was considered despicable and dishonorable, women enjoyed a wide latitude of movement; ergo, a woman could carry a torch to light up the enemy for her husband or carry the straw needed for her husband to burn down an enemy's house (Boehm, 100, 111). Although never obligated to kill, a woman who negated her "natural weakness" and fought like a man was revered more than her male counterpart, who was obliged to engage in revenge. Such women are celebrated in Montenegrin epic poetry (47).

Restoring one's honor through *krvna osveta* (blood revenge) was, upon occasion, taken a step further, by taking the head of the enemy. To ensure proper burial of the body required retrieval of the head. In *Land without Justice*, Milovan Djilas, himself a Montenegrin, relates an event in his family regarding head-hunting, which went beyond mere revenge. Not only did his grandfather, Aleksa Djilas, kill his enemy, he also cut out his heart, which, as might be expected, exacted a similar act by the dead man's family. To add insult to murder, Aleksa was summarily decapitated, his head literally thrown to the wolves. Reclamation of the head was analogous to the "retrieving of one's honor and pride, almost as though the man had not been slain" (15–16). Aleksa's daughter Stanojka fulfilled the assignment, but not without consequence. She was psychologically troubled for the duration of her life (16–17). Because of Western aversion to head-hunting, during the Balkan Wars, Montenegrins cut off the noses of their enemies rather than their heads (Durham 1928, 177–79).

* * *

Pacification of feuds, or "conflict management," was essential to the survival of tribal Montenegro. Through an ironic twist, feuding, the very practice to be controlled, was used as a tool to solve social problems, strengthening and uniting the people against the formidable Turks and other foreign invaders. Blood vendettas were frequently settled through marital alliances and "godfathering" (Vujačić, 60). Intratribal feuds were socially destructive, especially when they took place between the clan of a wife and that of her husband. Normal social activities were stressful for both parties, fearing the loss of kin. Such occurrences affected the economic fabric of the society, curtailing *moba* (communal participation in harvesting), for example. Once the impact of these social disruptions made itself felt, their containment became paramount, preventing repercussions in the tribe at large (Boehm, 181). Montenegro's tribal society and unabated struggle to remain free must be understood in the context of its violent past. It is equally important that it be lauded for the "moral probity, intelligence, and civility" of a "proud, fierce, and quite-unusual European tribal people" (246).

If truth be told, women—specifically, mothers of sons—were avid supporters of blood feuding, willing to surrender their offspring for tribal continuity. A warrior's death had deep moral consequence. Mothers of boys too young to carry guns moralized about the nobility of blood revenge, encouraging their participation when they came of age. A widow kept the "bloodied clothing" of her murdered husband as a constant reminder to her son that he must avenge him—failure to do so was dishonorable. As reinforcement, she admonished him daily, grieving and wailing in his presence. Not only was this provocation her moral duty, it was her right as a mother. But she likely exercised it because she had to in order to preserve the family's honor and good name. Her reproach of her son arose out of practical sense, the exigencies of communal daily life, which demanded that every family do its part in defending the country. Though fully prepared to accept her parental obligations, a mother might well secretly pray for their abolishment (Vujačić, 99–101).

Children had to learn the hard lessons of life in their formative years; if not, they would be ill-equipped to handle the psychological and physical demands of incredibly harsh Montenegro. Although no longer endemic, blood feuds have not ceased. According to a story related to me in 1990, one was then taking place in a town on the seacoast. For the previous two years the males in the family had been forced to remain behind the walls of their compound. The women worked to support the family, seeing to all of the chores outside the home. Whether it has since been resolved, I have no knowledge. If not, how long it will go on is anyone's guess.

Any public display of emotion, such as fear, joy, or grief—particularly grief for sons and husbands killed in battle—was considered a sign of weakness. An inadvertent indiscretion against the collective moral norm, or the slightest expression of indifference toward a public or private enemy, could cost a man his life. It was therefore essential that one's facial expressions, gestures, and speech be controlled (Gezeman, 144–45). Moderation in all aspects of behavior is critical, preached the ancient Greeks. Not so, proclaimed the Montenegrins: lack of extreme discipline diminishes one's dignity.

If excessive self-control is antithetic to a naturally violent race, how does one explain the Dinaric race? Gerhard Gezeman tells us that the more violent one is, the more self-restraint must be exercised (144). In a civilized society order is crucial, demanding mastery over natural animal instincts. Over the centuries, experience expunged from the "blood" of Montenegro those instincts unbefitting a civilized society. By listening to the "whisper of blood," they learned that molding nature to create harmony requires of each individual conscious limiting, directing, and building (150). In this Montenegro has triumphed.

∗   ∗   ∗

Double sexual standards are inextricably woven into the moral fabric of Montenegro, yet control over one's sexual urges is pivotal for both males and females—more so for females, as might be expected in any patriarchy. Young warriors are not only permitted sexual freedom, they are frequently "encouraged to ruin any maiden foolish enough to believe their promises of marriage" (Boehm, 46–47). In a conversation my son, Mark, had with a centenarian woman concerning dating a village girl and its potential consequences, she shrugged and said with a smirk, "Don't blame the hawk for naive chickens." Even extramarital sex was acceptable providing it did not in any way place the family in a financial bind. Sexual emancipation notwithstanding, there were certain drawbacks. For instance, should a male defile a maiden from a "good house," her father had every right to take his life or exact monetary compensation (72–73). On the other hand, a "good" man would marry a girl he violated, particularly if her family's honor was in the balance (101).

Females had no options in matters of sexual conduct. The preservation of a girl's virginity was so pivotal that extreme precautionary measures were taken to impede sexual malfeasance. A mother bathed her newborn daughter in cold water "to prevent her from becoming hot-blooded, making certain she remained self-controlled and docile" (Gezeman, 155). As she got older, she suppressed any outward sign of emotional discomfort to avoid being reproached: "What's the matter with you? Aren't you a girl?" Regarding an especially beautiful girl, the following aphorism speaks for itself: "A fire which can ignite an entire house must be carefully watched" (155). Since nothing short of virginity was accepted upon a "good" marriage, I was curious as to the verifiability of a bride's innocence. I learned that the morning after the marriage is consummated, the women in the household would casually glance at the sheets on which the married couple slept. Because evidence of blood is decisive proof of a bride's purity, a husband would be relatively forceful during penetration. One can only imagine the pain, stress, and embarrassment she endured. Even today public discussion about sex is taboo in Montenegro. Rarely, if ever, is it mentioned among family members. Women are also prohibited from using obscene language. Noteworthy is the fact that men are extraordinarily heedful about using obscenities in the presence of women.

An illegitimate birth, though rare, was thought to bring shame to the entire country. It was punishable by death, with the sentence carried out by the girl's parents (Aleksandrov, 374). Nonvirgins, those who miraculously survived, were relegated to marrying old men who needed sons or to the mentally ill. An alternative was to marry into another tribe, where the woman's reputation was unknown. Occasionally, a man took a strong, healthy "loose" woman from a respected family as his wife (Boehm, 71).

Even more profound is the following story told to me in Podgorica. The young mother of two sons and beautiful widow of one of three brothers living under the same roof, as is customary, indulged in sexual relations with one of the two remaining brothers. When the pair realized the woman was pregnant, they went to Albania, hoping there to abort the pregnancy. Had she attempted an abortion on her own or sought help with it locally, all those involved would have been ostracized at best. As it turned out, her pregnancy was too advanced, and they returned home. To preclude dishonoring the *bratstvo* (clan), a marriage contract was quickly arranged with an acquiescent bachelor three times her age, who happily pretended the child was of his own making.

* * *

Traditional patriarchies are also patrilineal societies, placing males in a position of unequivocal power. They are sole owners and inheritors of all material wealth. Primogeniture in a society valuing sons above all wealth is inconceivable, the youngest son being no less treasured than the oldest. In Montenegro, an unmarried woman and only survivor in a family need not leave her father's home until her death, when the property would be transferred to the nearest male kin. To remove her from her family home was considered inhumane, a reflection on the honor of the clan. But if such a woman decided to marry, the property was not hers to give to her husband, according to tribal law. Rather, it reverted to males of the same blood line, *deueloj krvi* (thick blood) (Vujačić, 53). According to national law, in a family with only daughters, property was equally divided among them, except for weapons, which were ceded to the nearest male kin (Bojović, 12).

Patrilineal practices resulted in the development of a cult of male superiority to an almost incomprehensible degree. The mere mention of a male's name evoked "fearful respect" from women, leading to female subservience, a distinct characteristic of the traditional society (Vujačić, 42). A Montenegrin woman exercised extreme caution so as to neither undermine her husband in public nor subvert his authority and manliness. Her public persona was to remain mute in his presence (93). Even young males had more authority in the home than did the oldest female (Alexandrov, 373). No woman dared to walk in front of her husband, though he may be the worst of men (Vujačić, 119). Beyond that, she never called him by name, instead using expressions such as *domaćin* (head of household) or *moj domaćin* (my head of household) (93).

A husband's word was law; his wife expected to react to his every word and action. He ruled; she served and obeyed. Taking orders from any woman was a form of emasculation for which no Montenegrin man would stand. The day Prince Danilo, King Nikola's son, introduced the practice of kissing the hand of his princess in the very early twentieth century, signaled, for Montenegrins, the end of the world as they knew it. Even when the princess gave permission to an old Montenegrin shepherd to let his sheep graze on her land he refused, swearing he would never obey any woman (Gezeman, 135). "The ideal of womanhood involved obedience and submission," subsequently, "the more submissively a woman" molded "her personality, the higher her reputation in the village" (Saltzman, 58). Montenegrin women "did not rebel against their position," rather "they helped to foster it by their behavior, by teaching their daughters submissive behavior and by ridiculing women who did not conform to this role" (58). In the process, they validated the men.

A woman had to be especially cautious if for any reason she suspected her husband of wrongdoing. The law of the land in 1855 required that a woman who undermined or demeaned her husband be put to death like any murderer. She could not, however, be killed by a gun, for he who carried a gun could use it only to defend himself (Danilo I, Code 73). Whether the law was carried out to the letter is difficult to say, but to broach a husband brought unduly harsh punishment. Suspicion on the part of the wife was counter to what is known as the "patriarchal marriage ethic," meaning that the husband's word was law, whether he treated her fairly or not (Vujačić, 119). Either way the woman was clearly in a no-win situation. In Montenegro, where the mode of communication to this day is often the metaphor, aphorisms proliferate: "Man criticizes and shouts at his wife all of his life and learns that it is the weaker one who shouts."

There has obviously been a deep-seated, albeit subliminal, awareness among men that the subjugation of women does not translate into their being the weaker sex. Therefore, exercising complete control over her is imperative. Njegoš, the poet with his hand on the pulse of the people, correctly character-izes the rights and freedom of a Montenegrin husband in terms of his relation-ship with his wife:

> When my wife asks where I have been today,
> I will tell her that I've been sowing salt.
> And woe to her if she does not believe!
> (*Mountain Wreath,* lines 812–13)

To go anywhere, including the home of her natal family, a wife required permission from her husband (119).

Women in Montenegro evoked greater sympathy from strangers than did men, whose harsh warrior countenance elicited more fear than compassion (Aleksandrov, 373). Manifestations of male idolization were evident in a woman's every act. For example, every time she passed a mature male on the road, she stepped to the side, head bowed, until he passed her. It was also customary for her to kiss the hand of a male guest and to remove and to put on his shoes. Cloaks or overcoats were clearly gender-distinguishable, lest the man mistakenly wear the wrong one, causing himself utter humiliation (Bojović, 10). With guests and frequently without guests, a woman did not sit at the table with men. Gender discrimination permeated every facet of life, and the church was no exception: males stood in front, before the altar; women in the back. Any public display of affection toward a wife was considered unnatural (10). Even in the privacy of their home, a husband never expressed any tenderness toward his wife, not out of cruelty but fear of public judgment. What love and affection she received came from her in-laws (Vujačić, 119). Eventually, her children became her principle motivation for living.

* * *

In warrior societies males develop aggressiveness, dominance, and a desire for victory. Montenegro is no exception. Individualism can be added comfort-ably to this list. As inductees in the new Yugoslav army (1918), Montenegrins refused to heed the accepted "count-off" practices of soldiers in line, for no Montenegrin could ever publicly declare himself as "second" or "third." To avoid such denigration, if a soldier called out "one," the Montenegrin next to him responded, "I, next to him," and so on (Jovanovich, x).

All warrior societies suppress women: Turks, Mongols, and Tartars. During his travels, Marco Polo noted that Tartar women not only worked in the home and in the fields but also managed all commercial activities, such as selling and buying, because the men knew nothing except how to fish, hunt, and go to war (Baković, 152–53). In Montenegro, "the superiority of a husband is essentially a public facade, practiced here more than any other Slavic or European group" (152). The narcissism evident in the Montenegrin male led him to seek more love than he was capable of giving. To a degree, he was self-sated. The combination of narcissism and aggressiveness empowered his solipsistic attitude toward women, and his wife in particular. As a result, no greater calamity could befall a Montenegrin than for his wife to ignore him (153). Paradoxically, continues psychiatrist Baković, though a Montenegrin might ignore his wife, he also saw her as a saint; he subjugated her because she was weak, and because she was weak, she was saintly and revered (147).

Conceding to the realities of life, the Montenegrin woman found her niche within her environment (Bojović, 10). In essence, both husband and wife created their own patriarchal world based on what was considered normal and moral (Vujačić, 119). On one hand, the marginalization of the Montenegrin woman cannot be refuted. On the other hand, she was markedly more protected and respected than women in many far more advanced societies. The women of Montenegro have suffered deprivation, but never degradation.

Despite male authority and its concomitant—the subjugation of women— civilized behavior between men and women was mandatory in Montenegro. A husband may not have behaved toward his wife in the same manner as would today's civilized man; however, pity the man who dared insult or demean the wife of a Montenegrin. When such a situation did occur, it was essential that the husband expunge his shame by defending his honor as a warrior and that of his wife as well (124). Vindication could take a variety of forms, from physical attacks to actual murder.

Never abandoned by blood relatives, no woman need tolerate insults or injustices from anyone, including her husband. Beside marrying a man's daughter, the husband also formed close ties with her family, creating a relationship based on mutual respect (Gezeman, 145). That the life of a Montenegrin woman is difficult cannot be contested, but she was never a "plaything in the hands of her husband," as happens in some very civilized lands (Baković, 148). Secure in the knowledge that no harm could come to her from any quarter, she could safely travel anywhere, even with strangers.

Scholars have conflicting views regarding woman's status in Montenegro. Following intensive analysis of this subject, Baković concludes that "she is the major pillar of the Montenegrin ethos" (148). When considering her contributions on myriad levels, she can be no less.

* * *

The work ethic in Montenegro was clearly defined for both sexes; deviation from its rigid rules was scandalous, principally for males. No man did "women's work," otherwise he was not to be considered "among men." Not surprisingly, most work was "women's work" (Bojović, 10). Female family relations of a warrior felt shame when he failed to meet the criteria of a hero. Should a woman find she could not complete her duties, she would sooner ask for assistance from a female neighbor than from her husband. Though a woman did most everything, there were a few tasks outside of her domain.

Montenegrin males have gained a reputation for being indolent, deservedly so to a degree. Nevertheless, had they had the luxury of work, they would have fulfilled their obligation. That was not a consideration, however, if life as they knew it was to endure. Independence and Montenegro are indistinguishable. If Montenegro is to be understood, it must be seen in that context. To protect their liberty and the land they had painfully acquired demanded constant vigilance, weapons at the ready. Consequently, a man was unable to do any type of outdoor work requiring bending or stooping, for to do so endangered him and his family. To ensure the safety of all, he must stand in an upright position with a broad view of the terrain, a loaded rifle by his side. During intermittent periods of peace, he did the physical work becoming a warrior.

In Montenegro arable land is at a premium. To uncover it from beneath huge boulders requires Herculean strength, as does the breaking of rocks to make fences for the protection of both people and animals. Such tasks fell to the males. When a man carried a burden, he carried it on his back, never his shoulders, freeing his head to observe his surroundings. Should an enemy appear, he could quickly dispose of it and use his weapon, which he always carried with him (Škerović, 263). Under ordinary circumstances, it was inappropriate for a man to carry a load on his back, much less a cradle. One of Prince Nikola's guards refused to pick up the prince's screaming child. Angered, the prince confronted the guard, who replied, "Why should I pick up your child if I don't pick up my own at home? That's a woman's job" (Gezeman, 134).

Rebecca West looks at the Montenegrin male work ethic from another standpoint. The "vainglory" of the Montenegrin negates any other possible characteristic, she writes, except "the cunning of the Homeric heroes," who resist all activity for fear of failure unbecoming a warrior. As a result, "Montenegrins are not interested in any kind of work," making it almost impossible "to fit them into the modern state of Yugoslavia" (1009). The only type of work that interests Montenegrins is "war," their "national industry" (Laffan, 47). Their way of life demanded a constant supply of warriors.

* * *

The motivating force behind matrimony was "to beget little heroes, who would not trouble to come out of their mothers' wombs were they not certain that they would grow up in heroism" (West, 1009). Marriage, children, ancestors, and descendants were the fundamental underpinnings of households, clans, tribes, and society in traditional Montenegro (Gezeman, 146). People married in adolescence. It was not uncommon for a 15- or 16-year-old male to marry a 13-year-old pubescent female. Some took even younger brides, consummating the union at maturity (Medaković, 64). King Nikola I (prince, 1860–1910; king, 1910–16) became engaged to Milena when he was 12 and she was half that age. While he studied in Paris, she lived with his family in Cetinje, and upon his return they were married—she just shy of 16, he 20 (Jovičević, 38, 40). In utero engagements were also standard. Two pregnant women frequently conspired to cement the relationships of their soon-to-be-born babies. Two boys would become *pobratimi* (blood brothers), and girls, *posestrime* (blood sisters). But if the infants were of the opposite sex, they would be engaged to be married (Aleksandrov, 373).

My great-grandmother Andjuša had just such an experience in 1858, the date of her birth and her engagement. (Working our way back chronologically, my mother and I came up with what we believe to be an accurate date, since no records exist.) Engaged in utero, she and her fiancé were 12 years old when they formally married. She left her *rod* (birth family) and went to her *dom* (husband's family). As a child, my mother lived with her grandmother, a lonely widow for many years, who loved to reminisce. For the first four years of her married life in her *dom* she and her husband played as children. On reaching 16, "something happened to him and he took me behind a rock," she told my mother, "and he went to war against the Turks, and I had a baby. A year later I was a widow, and soon after I buried my child."

Life in extended families, confined to one room, afforded little or no privacy. Therefore, most children were both conceived and born outside the home: in barns or fields. A parturient woman delivered her child under the most primitive conditions. A colleague detailed a typical childbirth in the time of the centenarians interviewed in this book. The pregnant woman was forced to walk back and forth in the shed where she would give birth. If she were fortunate enough, another woman, or women, would assist her should she be too exhausted or in too much in pain to walk by herself. Lying or sitting down was not permitted for fear the baby would not be able to exit, and a pile of straw was placed beneath the woman to prevent serious injury when it did emerge. Many women died from a lack of medical treatment for complicated deliveries.

A husband never assisted his wife with childbearing. More often than not, he left home several days prior to the birth, returning only when he heard his wife had delivered (Vukmanović, 226). Widowed fathers remarried at the earliest possible opportunity. In point of fact, childless widows could remarry with little trauma. A widow with children rarely remarried, however, because she had to leave her offspring behind and go with her new husband to her new *dom*. Children belonged to the father in every case. My great-grandmother, who was a childless widow living with her *rod*, remarried when she was around 18 years old and went to her new *dom*. She had four children with her new husband. By the time my mother came on the scene, her grandmother—or *Baba*—had lost her only son.

"In 1905," seeking a better life, "some sixty-seven hundred Montenegrins left their homeland, bound chiefly for North America" (Treadway, 4). *Baba* Andjuša's only son sought to join them. She pleaded with him not to leave her, but he threatened suicide should she deny him her blessing. Determined to fulfill his threat, he took the gun hanging on the wall (found in every Montenegrin home). As she attempted to wrest it from him, it fired, taking off her thumb. He boarded the ship but never made it to America. Having developed a urinary tract infection and being too embarrassed to seek medical care, he died and was buried at sea.

For many years she did not know that her *jedinac* (only son) was dead. Those who received letters from America pretended they were from him and read them to her, creating a fictitious story about his experiences in his new land. Being illiterate, she had no way of knowing the truth, until it became troublesome to shield it from her. Hearing what is a mother's worst nightmare, she reacted in accordance with the grieving customs of her culture, never shedding a tear, remaining poised and stoic. Behaving otherwise would bring dishonor to both family and clan.

A mother never publicly grieves for her son. My mother tells me that her grandmother arose in the wee hours of the morning, went up to a rock quite a distance from her house, and sat there, wailing at the top of her lungs, calling out her son's name. The echo of her voice rolling over the mountains would awaken my mother, who was then around six years old. Returning several hours later and asked where she had been, my great-grandmother made up some story about having to gather the sheep left out the night before. Despite her troubled life, she lived to be 102 years old. There are many *babe* in Montenegro with as many sad narratives, some of which are between the covers of this book.

Few societies believe in the manifestly inherited qualities of different individuals as do Montenegrins: "From wherever is your wife, so are your children" (Gezeman, 146–47). The science of selective mating is an age-old practice in Montenegro. To appreciate the value of eugenics, one need only look at the offspring of Princess Jelena (1872–1952), the beautiful, tall, stately daughter of Prince Nikola, and her conspicuously short husband, Prince Victor Emmanuel of Savoy and future king of Italy. It was hoped that a marital arrangement "with a well-born princess from the mountains would renew the Italian royal line, already biologically endangered by inter-marriages within the Savoy family" (Jovičević, 167). It did just that.

* * *

In old Montenegro, selecting a bride entailed painstaking research by members of the groom's family. What they sought was a flawless reputation, hers and that of her family. A "good house"—not the bride's personal appearance—was crucial. Whether they saw her in person mattered little. Reputations are formed over generations of bravery, so her family's history, going back at least 100 years, was the determining factor in the selection process (Gezeman, 148–49). The maxim "Marry from nobodies and you'll have nobodies around your hearth" precisely encapsulates the consequences of marrying from a "weak house," reinforcing the notion that sons take after maternal grandfathers and uncles (Vujačić, 142). Once the groom's relations were satisfied that they had found the right girl for him, they asked her father for her hand in marriage. Her sentiments were of no consequence. Three days prior to the wedding ceremony, the future groom must notify his local priest that he, with the "consent" of his future bride, agrees to marry. Notwithstanding constitutional law, what takes place in actual practice, if we are to believe the literature and the women in this study, is that the future bride—despite being given the option of refusing to accept her family's choice of husband—rarely contests their decision.

Both young people come to their wedding as strangers. The bride, in fact, is not simply wrested from the bosom of her parents. Marriage was a sacred fusion of two respected families, not a casual exchange of goods, a practice for which Montenegrins condemned their enemy, the Turks, as expressed by Njegoš: "No wedding at all is their old custom. Instead, they make some kind of a contract, as if they are renting half a cow. They do not count women as family, but they treat them like purchased slaves instead. And they tell you, 'Woman is to a man like some sweet fruit or a piece of roast lamb. While she is that, you may keep her at home; when she is not, throw her out on the street!' " (*Mountain Wreath,* lines 1769–77). Sensitive to the concerns of the bride, and her parents in particular, the groom's wedding party, in the presence of both, begins the traditional ritual of easing the bride's exit from her family and into her new home.

In a detailed study, G. Medaković describes the activities of a traditional wedding day. On the day of the prearranged wedding, a party of males from the groom's family, perhaps 60 to 100 men, sets out to collect the bride and deliver her to the groom's village church, where she will be married. The main witnesses are generally the groom's maternal and paternal relatives: *stari svat* (senior), usually the groom's uncle; *djeveri, lijevi i desni* (groom's two brothers, the left one and the right one); *prvienac* (leader of the bridal procession); *barjaktar* (flag bearer, a son of the groom's maternal uncle); *kum* (best man); and *vojvoda* (groom's brother-in-law). All spend the night before the wedding at the house of the groom, each firing his gun as he arrives. If there is insufficient room they are distributed throughout the groom's *bratstva* (blood relatives). Relatives have already gathered to greet them. Upon entering the house, their weapons are taken by the groom or some other member of the household (Medaković, 64).

After lunch on the day of the wedding, the wedding party, carrying flasks of wine that they offer to those they meet on the road, leaves to pick up the bride, who also has a *prvienac* and a *barjaktar*. As the groom's wedding party nears the bride's house, the men begin to dance, signaling the bride's brother and her *prvienac* to bring out their flag. The groom's *prvienac* and *barjaktar* separate from the group and meet with those of the bride, and the two *barjaktari* and *prvienci* meet. All four dance: *barjaktar* with *barjaktar*, *prvienac* with *prvienac*. Subsequently, they fire their guns, and both pairs embrace. After the *barjaktari* place both flags in front of the house or on it, the witnesses enter in the order in which they walked; weapons are taken and hung on the wall.

The entire group stands at the table before a fully prepared meal, sitting down in order of importance: at the head of the table, the groom's *stari svat* and his witnesses; to his left, the bride's *stari svat* and her witnesses. Toasts begin. Wrapped in a handkerchief are *opanke* (peasant shoes), with a coin in one, which the *djever* hands to the bride's brother. *Opanke* in hand, he enters the room where his sister waits, while several women prepare to dress her. He places the *opanke* on the tip of her toes, which she herself slips on (Medaković, 64). Donning the *opanke* initiates the severing of ties to her natal home and the bonding with her new family. After she removes all but her long blouse and petticoat, her brother assists her with her wedding dress, pulling it just over her head until it touches her shoulders. He then takes the cap from her head (worn solely by unmarried girls), throws it under his feet, and exits the room (64). The removal of her cap symbolizes the end of girlhood and imminent passage into wifehood.

The women continue dressing the bride, placing two white scarves on her head, secured with two hairpins. That morning she has bathed with scented soap, put her hair in two braids and slipped an apple or two in her bosom. The apple will become part of a fertility ritual she will perform as a bride prior to entering her husband's home for the first time. In the interim, her father presents the wedding party with handkerchiefs, asking them whether they are satisfied with their gifts. All respond in the positive, settle down, and continue eating and drinking. Finally, upon the demand of the groom's *stari svat*, "Give us the girl!" she is brought out on her brother's arm. One *djever* says, "Give me the girl!" to which her brother responds, " I will not, until you give me a gift." "What can I give you?" he asks. "You can give me a cartridge," answers the brother, which he will fire as the bride departs for her new home (Medaković, 64).

At that moment, both right and left *djeveri* take the bride by the arm, so no member of her family touches her. This ritual begins the process of assuring the bride that she will be honored and protected in her *dom* as if she were a sister. Touching her would have been scandalous, misconstrued as a sign that the bride's family is not entirely confident in their daughter's future family. The right-hand *djever* takes the bride over to the groom's *stari svat*, who places a ring on her finger, she bowing and kissing his hand. He then escorts her around the table, she stopping to kiss the hand of the groom's *svatovi* (Medaković, 65–67). The blessings commence.

The bride's father offers the first blessing:

> May God give you four sons and two daughters,
> first the daughters, then sons, so that the two evils will never meet.

Metaphorically, the father hopes that, first, she will have children of both sexes. If the daughters are born first, they will marry and be out of the house before the sons marry and bring their wives into the home. Thus, the sisters-in-law will not have the opportunity to cause dissension in the home. Subsequently, the mother tenders her blessings:

> Go with God, my daughter. I can do no more for you.
> So, may God grant you all that I wish for you.

The bride's *stari svat* proposes the final toast:

> Go with God, girl. Have a safe trip, so that those
> in your *dom* can brag about having the best girl,
> the most fortunate and honorable. What more
>   can we say?
> What she sows she shall reap. To your health,
>   brothers!

Upon orders from the groom's *stari svat*—"On your feet *svatovi;* it's time to go"—they depart in the order in which they entered the house. As they leave, they are handed their loaded weapons, which they fire a distance from the house, and then only once. By this time, her brother has climbed up on a tree limb or on the roof of the house, calling his sister by name, saying, "Go with God," and firing his gun. Her *djeveri*, walking on either side of her, observe carefully to see whether she turns around. The slightest indication, perhaps a facial twitch, that she yearns for a final glance at her brother would be humiliating, for then her progeny indeed would take after their maternal uncle (Medaković, 69).

From the moment she exits the home of her parents, she becomes a member of a family of strangers, to whom she, too, is an alien. She will now assume her rightful place in society, tending to a *"tudja večera"*—a stranger's supper—a role for which she has prepared all of her life (Gezeman, 155). While growing up a girl was constantly reminded that her real home was not the one where she was born but that of her *dom*, the one she would share with her husband and his family. In essence, the home of her parents was an interim home, a place where she would mature and learn how to become a respected and contributing member of a stranger's home and family. Once in her *dom*, she would prepare the supper, the central meal around which the entire extended family gathered; her serving of the supper was ostensibly a metaphor for her having to attend the needs of her new, extended family for the remainder of her life.

Her parents expected nothing from her while she was in their care except that she maintain a pristine reputation and that she someday marry. No member of her family will attend the church wedding. Still, a respected sociological study asserts that the bride never severed relations with her family or was made to believe that she no longer belonged to them. She remained concerned with the reputations of her new family and her birth family, owing allegiance to both (Bojović, 11).

When the wedding party arrives at the church in the groom's village, the best man leaves to escort the groom to the church. Before leaving his house, however, the groom asks his parents for their blessings, kissing their hands. Women do not attend the church service. Following the ceremony, the bride, head bowed, exits the church escorted by her *djeveri*, never having glanced at her new husband. In front of the church, members of the wedding party have a drink and fire their guns, singing as they walk to the groom's house. His entire clan anxiously awaits them. The groom's mother, holding a small boy in her arms, welcomes the guests. Before the threshold lies a handmade blanket or rug. The bride takes the child into her arms, steps on the blanket or rug, and enters the house, presenting the child with a pair of *opanke*, a coin in each one (Medaković, 69).

This ritual, like many others, has enormous significance in a society consumed with male progeny (69). Prior to taking the child and entering the house, the bride tosses the apples she has carried in her bosom over the roof of her new home, trusting that they, too, will bless her with many children, preferably males. It was also customary to place weapons under the rug, for then "she was the more likely to bear a warrior" (Durham, 1928, 208). During all of these ceremonial rites, the right-hand *djever* never leaves her side, sitting with her at the head of a sumptuous table and giving her food and drink (70). She is for the first and last time in her life served food by a male.

The *djever*, as brother of the groom, has one final responsibility: He, not the husband, spends the first wedding night sleeping with the bride, both fully clothed. This ritual is designed to appease an apprehensive bride compelled to sleep with a strange man in an alien environment, as preparation for the eventual bedding down with her husband—a stranger—and consummation. It also serves as reassurance to both the bride and her natal family that this new home is no less a sanctuary than the home in which she was born. Furthermore, the nuptial period between wedding and consummation affords her time to acclimate to a foreign milieu prior to her first, at best traumatic, sexual experience. Should her brother-in-law make the slightest sexual over-ture, even in jest, his life could be forfeited, for in doing so he has shown disrespect for the bride and her family, as well as for his family and the groom, his brother. The following night she might sleep with her husband's sister or some other female. "To defer the consummation of the marriage . . . was considered honorable. . . . The longer the more honorable . . . sometimes deferred for a year or more." The explanation offered for this practice was that the bride was *stidna*, or shy (Durham 1928, 208). I must take exception, however, to Durham's assertion that the "custom of sleeping with the *djeveri* after the marriage ceremony was extinct in Montenegro" by the turn of the century (208). From my conversations with women in 1990, I learned that this convention was in effect at least up until World War II, and beyond in many villages.

Customarily, on the third day the bride's mother, brother, and uncle pay her a visit, bringing with them her clothing and a scented bar of soap as a gift for each of the women. The groom receives a vest, socks, and garters. Frequently traveling from a great distance, they may stay for several days. Several weeks later the bride visits her family, accompanied not by her hus-band but by her two *djeveri*. When they first escorted her from her family's home to that of her husband, they walked on either side of her. Once married, her position has been altered significantly. She is now obliged to walk behind them and every other man, including her husband. While at the home of her parents, she shares a bed with both men, all fully clothed, once more confirm-ing their esteem for a new sister-in-law and family member (Durham 1928, 70).

The bride does not sleep with her husband until she is given permission to do so by one of the older women in the household. At that time, a small alcove in the only room in the house is set aside for the couple, possibly separated by a curtain for privacy in a space occupied by the entire family. Through my discussions with several people, I discovered that it was com-monplace for a husband to cover the face of his wife with a black opaque scarf when having sex, to shield her from feeling shame. None of the women in this study admitted to having such an experience, which does not rule out the possibility that they did have it. The sooner the new bride gives birth, the sooner she will enjoy the respect accompanying motherhood—her rite of passage. A son brings her that honor. Having daughters exclusively diminishes her position, though not quite to the extent that it would if she were childless.

The new bride undergoes rigorous "testing" by her new family. Her status in the home depends on the whims of her mother-in-law. All women in traditional Montenegro are responsible to the wife of the *starešina* (head of the household). A woman's submissive role alters with age, creating a new "pecking order"; she has earned the right to give orders to the younger women in the house (Saltzman, 57).

By the middle of the nineteenth century, the society began to accept national rather than tribal laws, and the position of women improved. Even males were punishable by law. Around the 1880s, abused women began to avail themselves of the laws governing their lives, whereas in earlier years they endured in silence. Naturally, males resisted the newfound liberation of women, finding it antithetic to the attitudes regarding the role of women formulated over the centuries. Undeterred by such opposition, more and more women sought divorces in the court in Cetinje. Having been inculcated with centuries-old tribal practices, a man occasionally killed his wife in court in the course of a trial, despite the new laws (Bojović, Code 11).

Under these laws, a man could divorce his wife if she had stolen from him for a third time, at which time he could legally remarry, while she was compelled to remain single. For the first two times she was caught stealing from her husband, her punishment was incarceration (Danilo I, Code 77). A husband could also divorce his wife for having bad breath. In any case, he would first have to consult with his relatives (Vujačić, 135).

Divorce could not be granted to a couple on grounds of incompatibility. In such cases, the couple was permitted to live separately. He is obliged to support her, and neither could remarry while one of them is alive (Danilo I, Code 75). There is an exception to this law, however. If the wife caused her husband any provocation while the couple was separated, he was granted a divorce and absolved of all spousal support (Code 76). Another prerogative also came his way in the event of her infidelity: a cuckolded husband could cut her nose off if he so chose (Durham 1928, 213). Laws requiring the flogging or stoning of women were generally never carried out, often substituted by jail sentences. Punishment by death was similarly replaced by imprisonment (Bogišić, 139–40). Change notwithstanding, Montenegrins continued to live according to the same tribal beliefs they had held for untold generations.

* * *

The stabilizing factor in all Montenegrin matrimony was love of family and responsibility to the family. So intense was the yearning for progeny that it was difficult to find a similar passion in other societies. The longing for sons was considered simply "human" and "God given" (Vujačić, 128). With such an obsession, it is patently clear why wedlock without issue was seen as lacking a firm foundation. Fecundity extended far beyond personal fulfillment and the instinctive drive for having one's own family. It was the quintessential motivation for living a civilized, patriarchal life. Offspring were thought to enrich the relationship between husband and wife in terms of mutual love, respect, and tolerance. Not surprisingly, the wife and not the husband was faulted when there was no issue. Since children were central factors in a family, an infertile wife could be sent back to her birth family, a practice lasting throughout the traditional period. In the middle of the nineteenth century, laws were introduced forbidding such practices (Vujačić, 129). As in many other instances, patriarchal tendencies die hard; some prevail in rural Montenegro today.

Divorcing a woman because she was sterile could trigger a blood feud. To avoid such an occurrence, a barren wife would *voluntarily* choose to leave her husband, thus freeing him of culpability and enabling him to take another wife (Vujačić, 130). In an issueless union, the husband became a bigamist. Though perfectly legitimate, this act occurred only in dire circumstances and was carried out with high moral awareness and consultation with church and local authorities (131). I have not heard of such incidents in today's Montenegro, but the idea cannot be ruled out in remote, isolated villages.

The basic justification for bigamy was located in the Montenegrin male's obsession with having sons. Nor was the woman excluded from this fixation. A woman with a good husband was especially desirous that he have sons, that his "flame not be extinguished" (Vujačić, 133). On this basis, a barren wife might bring into the house another woman to bear her husband's children, and she, under her own initiative and that of her husband, would remain in the house as "aunt" or "godmother" (115). Frequently, these alliances receive blessings from the *pop*, as long as there was no interference from the bishop in Cetinje (Gezeman, 156). Although the priest might sanction the new union, the first one was not legally dissolved, nor was the husband legally married to the second woman. Once again, tribal law superseded all other laws.

So important were sons that a father with only daughters considered himself to be without offspring. A home without males loses its surname, its patrilineal patron saint, and "hearth"; there will be no one to uphold the traditions of home and clan (Vujačić, 115). Gezeman states that a "happy childbirth" meant the birth of a son. A man without a son felt betrayed, lost and neglected, becoming bitter and sadistic toward those with male offspring. He was to be feared. One was wary of his curses, which were thought to have evil magical powers over those more fortunate. Believing that the sonless man's home had been punished by God, other parents prayed they would not suffer the same fate: "I hope my house is never overturned like his," or "I hope my candle does not burn out like his." Having only one son was regarded as having no sons; having two was regarded as having one, because at least half of the males in a household would be slain in war (156).

A male child was welcomed with joy and gunfire: "A new man has arrived on Earth who will defend his country." Legend had it that on the birth of a male child, a pistol was placed next to him, on his pillow. This was his first toy (Alexandrov, 370). Citing a personal example, on the way to an interview I asked my guide whether he knew of my husband's family, and he remarked, "Oh yes, the Milichs had five guns [my husband's grandfather and his sons]. In the old days, many great swordsmen came from their clan."

Mothers in old Montenegro enjoyed a markedly higher degree of respect than did childless women. Not surprisingly, they were the most celebrated (Vujačić, 131). Mothers and sisters were credited by society for raising their sons and brothers as warriors in the strict sense of the patriarchy: to be brave and honorable. Elder males still speak proudly and movingly of such women (Gezeman, 132). Modern Montenegrin women are still the pillars of their families, within a relatively intact patriarchy.

Among Montenegrin males there existed an indisputably distinct phenomenon that Dr. Baković calls "mother cult," a perfectly appropriate term for this culture (149). An environment with a mother as sole tutor, often a war widow, generates ideal conditions for the development of a strong oedipal complex. In adult Montenegrin males, the oedipal complex was transformed into a symbiotic projection of love, respect, consideration, and obedience toward mothers, rarely seen to such a degree in other cultures (151). This is not to say that some women are not resentful of a husband's attention to his mother. Even so, their sons will continue in the footsteps of those males who came before them; to do otherwise is to betray tradition.

A mother taught her offspring that their father, not she, was paramount; therefore, the Montenegrin woman was not a castrating mother, continues Baković. She idealized, exalted, and swore by her husband, doing everything in his name, even frightening the children with him, thus upholding his persona as the preeminent authority in the home, dead or alive (156–57). Mothers gave their children the best education available. Though illiterate, they, with or without husbands, remained their children's best teachers, greatest critics, and most steadfast sources of support (157). Under a mother's tutoring, children would grow into healthy and well-adjusted adults. It is said that after the death of a father a person matures, after the death of a mother one ages. While mother lives, children remain young; a mother's love is an elixir (152). It was the son in Montenegro, born in joy and celebration, who most deeply mourned the loss of the mother.

* * *

The greatest curse for a Montenegrin woman was that she came into the world as female, crying, "My God, Mother, why did you give birth to me?" (Pajević, 439, 442). The birth of a girl brought sadness into the family; everyone felt a misfortune had been brought into the home. Perhaps the family was distraught because its members knew her destiny would be one of grief and deprivation. Whatever the case, females were considered bad omens in the house. Blessed was the woman who gave birth to sons. In a home with sons, a daughter was less conspicuous.

All this antifemale feeling notwithstanding, girls were loved, and by no one more than their brothers, whom they in turn were prepared to defend with their lives. Brothers were extremely protective of their sisters. "The affection brothers held for their sisters frequently acted as a deterrent to husbands whose abuses might otherwise have been excessive" (Simić, 91). The women in this study cried and spoke movingly only when making reference to the deaths of their brothers. No record appears of a sister having killed her brother, though brothers have killed sisters, particularly in cases where she brought dishonor to the family (for example, an out-of-wedlock pregnancy). Vindication of the family name fell to him. Baković speaks of the implicit disparity between a man's open love and respect for his mother and the sensitivity he felt for his sister and daughter, which he concealed (147).

A father was embarrassed at not producing a son to defend his country, apologetic for the birth of a daughter, "Forgive me, a daughter was born to me" (Alexandrov, 371). When asked how many children he had, he might say, "three sons and, if you'll forgive me, three *children*." For that matter, so might a woman say something similar. However it was said, the fact of the apology for a daughter was consistent. The father either paid minimal attention to her or ignored her completely. Her upbringing and education were of no concern to him.

In these, as in all other matters concerning the home, the mother took full responsibility, training her in the principles of patriarchal life and the proper behavior becoming a woman. Since her primary goal in life was to be married, her first lesson in modesty was to prepare for that event, when she became the pillar, the "soul," of another family (Vujačić, 124). Mothers served as role models for daughters, who learned more through observation than by words (99).

* * *

Ethnographers write about the importance of women in times of war. Montenegrin mothers frequently took their daughters with them to the battlefield to see fathers, brothers, and other male relatives, bringing with them food and clothing for the men. With every male at war, women were obliged to do all the farming and household chores, completing them with great speed so that they could quickly reach the battlefield to lend support and encouragement to the men. Protected from being shot or killed by Montenegrin and Turkish tribal law, women confidently took munitions to the front, leading mules carrying gunpowder and lead.

After the battle, they searched for their men, offering soldiers water and brandy, which they always brought with them. When meeting a wounded soldier, the woman often said, "*Srećna ti rana*" (Happy and fortunate is your wound; metaphorically, his badge of courage and good fortune in having survived to fight again). Should she come across a dead relative, she would be overwhelmed by grief, falling on the corpse, kissing and hugging it, wailing from the deepest chasms of her mangled heart.

Prior to burial, she would collect his weapon, medals, hat, bloodied clothing, and all other belongings. If he were her husband, she would use these items as a teaching tool for her children, to illustrate how their brave father had sacrificed his life for their liberty. Some women were armed and fought alongside the men. Their names and deeds are preserved in Montenegrin history (Bojović, 14).

Following such battles one could see many men, wounded and otherwise, wearily wending their way home, with women weeping and calling out the names of their dead (Aleksandrov, 378–79). As the weary and injured entered their villages, they were met by *tužbalice* (professional female mourners), wailing as the villagers followed them to their homes. There, the dead man's clothing was spread out on a long table for all to see, arranged in such a way that the body would appear to be lying there (Pajević, 453). *Tužbalice* went from house to house wherever there was a funeral. So moving and sad was their sound that one would do anything to escape it (455). Until recently, women scratched their faces and drew blood at the funeral of loved ones as a sign of insufferable grief—mostly young women for their fathers or their brothers (Aleksandrov, 380).

Sociologist Vujačić states that the rights of a *tužbalica* extended far beyond mere mourning. She had the right to judge events and men, thus gaining social position and the power to express herself as mother, wife, sister, or friend in pain and suffering. In the role of educator, she admonished people to protect and to fulfill familial, tribal, and national ideals. In epic poetry, she is depicted as one who inspires warriors to continue their struggle for autonomy. Her words are as significant as those of men—perhaps more so (150).

Women *nariču* (wail) in such a way that one unfamiliar with the custom would think they are singing. They composed their own sad songs while working in the fields (Nenadović, 74). During periods of war, one could hear no other songs except those having to do with wailing (75), repeatedly interspersed with the word *kuku*, which led the singer to be mistaken for a *kukavica* (cuckoo bird) (75–77).

Though the uninitiated might find many of the tribal practices of Montenegro primitive and distressing, it is essential that they be viewed in the context of a traditional warrior society—original and unpolluted. Entering the third millennium A.D., much of tribal Montenegro lingers on as a living reflection of prefeudal Europe.

* * *

The bravery and honor of Montenegrin warriors is well documented. The world, however, knows little about those who gave life, who nurtured and educated those warriors, who worked from the cradle to the grave (Škerović, 370). Most of the studies of women in Montenegro have never been translated and published in other parts of the world. The portrait of a Montenegrin woman presented in these works, written almost exclusively by men, is corroborated by the self-perceived social experiences of the women in this study. That is to say, ethnic studies neither repudiate nor diminish the hardships of the female population. What literature does, and does very well, is idealize two specific stages of a woman's life: the innocence and beauty of young unmarried womanhood and the sanctity of motherhood. More to the point, among social scientists there is unanimous recognition of the incalculable contribution made by women to the preservation of a society whose central purpose has been to maintain its identity and sovereignty, encapsulated in a Montenegrin adage: A house does not rest on the ground, it rests on a woman.

Čojstvo i junaštvo—honor and heroism—are the preeminent building blocks of Montenegro. All else is inconsequential and fraudulent. From the compelling integrity of the women's stories told in this volume, much of the history of *Crna Gora* can be extrapolated. What they offer is an honest picture of reality, hardly theirs exclusively; it is the comprehensive reality of a self-contained mountain people. In fact, in their conscious conceptualization of their world lies the history of how all Montenegrins coped with a carefully circumscribed, exogamous social order—an order based more on accepted, strictly enforced tribal decrees than on written, national laws.

From a twentieth-century Western perspective, the traditional Montenegrin woman may be viewed as enslaved and unfulfilled. It is true that she lived under rigid constraints in an androcentric environment. Montenegro also made severe demands on its men, who at all times were expected to behave as brave and honorable warriors. In fact, the Montenegrin woman will be the first to admit that her life was one of toil and tragedy, wherein there was rarely a good day. This once unwelcome child became, as mother, the foundation of another family, to whom she selflessly dedicated her life. From her loins came the warriors who secured the freedom and survival of a people.

Without her physiological propensity, the future of the tribe—the child—could not be born. For that she was venerated, and perhaps prevented from succumbing to the hardships of life. She was comforted by the knowledge that her life was not unique, that she lived in a homogeneous community in which no woman's life differed from hers. Competition with and influences from sources external to her "hermetically sealed" world were similarly nonexistent. Within the patriarchal limitations imposed upon her she found self-fulfillment in the role of a good mother and respected wife and daughter-in-law; above all, she found it in raising warrior sons. An ancient Montenegrin proverb speaks for her, and for all Montenegrins: Suffering is our communal tragedy; heroism is our communal wealth; as long as we share these things, Montenegro will be one.

Let's now listen as the 100-year-old female voices of Montenegro take us across time into their tribal world.

PART I

Sons and Brothers: Death in the Midst of Death

Montenegro in the 1990s.

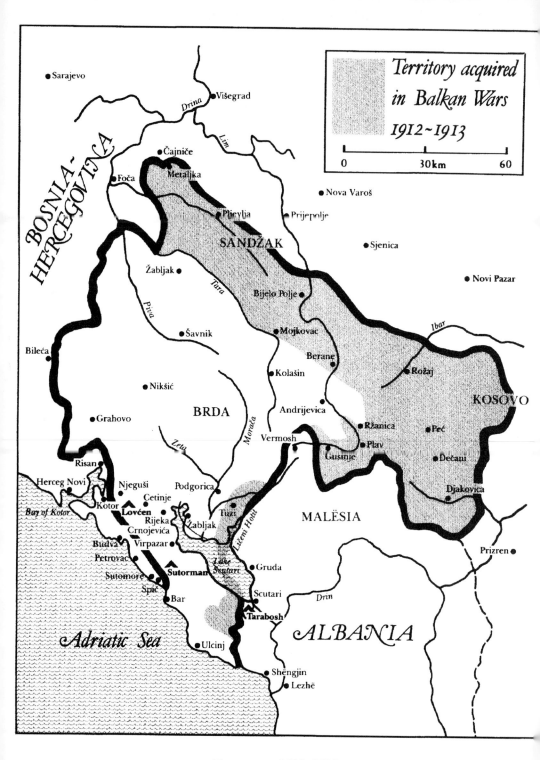

Montenegro, 1908–1914.

Petar II Petrović Njegoš (1811–1851). Almost seven feet tall, he was prince bishop of Montenegro from 1830 to 1851. He is Montenegro's most celebrated poet. As ruler he was known as Vladika Rade (Bishop Rade); as poet, Njegoš.

Nikola (1841–1921) ruled Montenegro as prince from 1860 to 1910 and as king from 1910 to his exile in 1916, when Montenegro was incorporated into Yugoslavia. Until his death in 1921 he resided in Italy, where his daughter Jelena reigned as queen with the Italian king Victor Emmanuel III.

King Nikola surrounded by his queen, Milena, and their children and their children's spouses. Nikola was known as the "father-in-law of Europe" because he married his daughters into its royal houses: Savoy, Romanov, Battenberg, Karadjorgević. The character Prince Danilo in Franz Lehár's operetta *The Merry Widow* is said to have been based on the Montenegrin prince Danilo (back row, fifth from left).

TRADITIONAL MONTENEGRO

Montenegrin woman carrying a load on her back. Her husband remains upright, shouldering a rifle to protect her and their family. Although the enemy could be another tribe, more often they were Ottoman Turks or Muslim Slavs.

Montenegrin woman caring for her child and her husband's guns.

Some women took active roles on the battlefield, a fact that is honored and celebrated in Montenegro's epic poetry. It was considered dishonorable for a man to retaliate against them.

Andrijevica, a village in northern Montenegro. *Courtesy of Serb World U.S.A.*

Rijeka Crnojevića, Montenegro. The Jovičević (the author's maternal family) ancestral home was originally owned by the royal family, and then served as a tavern. The bridge's arches were used as gallows by those who controlled the town, whether Montenegrins or Turks. Half a century after Gutenberg perfected the movable-type printing press in 1454, the world's second press was operating on a hill across from the bridge. *Mark W. Milich.*

A house in the Brda region of northern Montenegro.

Three generations of a traditional Montenegrin family.

Wedding portrait of Jovanka and Jovan Masanovich, parents of the author. Bride wears traditional national dress. Bridegroom wears western attire, having lived in the United States many years prior to his marriage in Montenegro. The Masanoviches left for America following the wedding.

In the remote mountain village of Smrduša, a guslar is reciting a heroic epic poem accompanying himself on a traditional Montenegrin instrument, a hand-carved gusle, strung with a single hank of horsehair and bowed. Its tones can still be heard throughout the Montenegrin mountains deep into the night.
Wallace M. Milich.

One of the eldest members of the Milić clan at 103 in 1968, at that time one of the few surviving centenarian males in Montenegro, wearing traditional national attire. He has a vintage Colt revolver in his sash.
Wallace M. Milich.

If a mother is as young as she is good without regard to her age, then before
us in this wooden coffin headed toward eternal nothingness is young,
beautiful Dobrota. The black cloth which you put on at age fourteen—black
is the sail without wind for your departure. You have left behind a wide and
deep trail: five sons, two daughters, twenty-four grandchildren and four
great-grandchildren—an entire tribe under a sooty helmet. One more thing,
dear mother: to your sons who wrote and edited books, you were the best and
most demanding of editors—the only one we feared.
—Son's eulogy at mother's grave, from Todor Baković's Depresivni
Optimizam Crnogoraca

The one constant in the lives of Montenegrin women is unnatural, premature death: death of husbands, death of children, death of brothers. Understandably, all losses have enormous impact on their psyches, particularly the death of a male child or the death of a brother at any stage of life and under any condition. All are mourned, but in significantly different ways.

A husband's death exacts limited emotion on the part of the wife. Most women in this study said they grieved for their husbands for a short while, some not at all, accepting his death as the natural evolution of life. Despite arranged marriages, it seems unlikely that some women did not love their husbands. So why prohibit articulation of genuine grief for a mate? The literature on this subject is vague. One reason may be that a wife's behavior toward her husband's death is an extension of the tone set in the early stages of her marriage, a time when she is restricted from having all but minimal contact with him. Any overt or covert gesture may be construed as erotic, which is totally unacceptable in a warrior patriarchy. Similarly, excessive grieving for a husband may be inferred as indicative of a wife ostensibly lamenting the absence of a sex partner—unbecoming behavior at *all* times. Paradoxically, whatever the degree of sorrow expressed for a husband in public, be it great or small, is entirely inappropriate when grieving for a son.

A son is mourned privately. This behavior is intended to enforce the stoicism of mothers in a society to which they proudly contribute warriors. Any public demonstration of suffering reflects weakness of character, the inability to endure the unendurable. The slightest suggestion of bereavement on her part is unbefitting a mother and maligns the family name. Her agony is exacerbated immeasurably when surrounded by women, family and professional mourners, all in varying stages of hysteria. I observed such a mother and remain in awe of her forbearance. Conversely, a brother's death releases a public outpouring of overwhelming grief.

When recalling the deaths of brothers, women weep inconsolably, without constraint or inhibition. It is the one tragedy in their lives for which public expressions of sorrow are condoned and expected; indeed, they are limitless. Self-mutilation—pulling out one's hair and pounding the chest with a fist—

is pervasive, particularly in rural areas. Sisters yearn to join brothers by attempting to jump into their graves. A sister will joyfully sacrifice her life for her brother. The rationale for this behavior is unclear, although literature is replete with tales of a sister's boundless love for her brother. Montenegrin women learn self-control in early childhood. As a result, by adulthood they have become masters at suppressing their feelings, knowing that the society neither fully acknowledges their existence nor provides an outlet for their emotions. It is possible—though mere conjecture—that the mourning of a brother, in some convoluted way, offers relief from a life of repressed emotions. I witnessed a young woman in her 20s in near hysteria, losing consciousness periodically, at the funeral of her 96-year-old great-grandfather. Had he been a brother, one can only imagine what might have taken place.

LJUBICA

Ljubica, somewhere between the ages of 112 and 115, came into my life through one of her city relatives, who saw me in a TV interview concerning my search for centenarian women. Within several days, I was informed by the History Institute of Crna Gora that a gentleman who had a female relative well over the age of 100 had called. I telephoned him, and we made arrangements to visit her. She lives in one of those painterly settings, high on a hill, in a valley surrounded by snow-capped mountains.

To get to her house in the Brda region from Podgorica, the driver, coordinator, and I traveled for several hours on a clear, sun-drenched though chilly spring day, through breathtaking canyons along the Morača River, until we reached an unpaved road. Undaunted in his reliable Mercedes, our driver continued on the secondary road for several kilometers before being forced to stop at the side of a mountain and the end of the road. My coordinator pointed to our destination: a house, a speck on the horizon, just a vague outline on the top of a steep hill.

The coordinator and I walked toward the house, leaving the driver behind. On our descent—the terrain consists of alpine-like hills and deep vales—we crossed a steadily flowing stream, stepping on various logs and rocks to get to the other side, sometimes slipping off and into the water. Once across, we began our ascent to Ljubica's house, meeting up with a tall, slender, energetic, middle-aged woman tending sheep while drawing wool on a distaff. She greeted us, inquiring as to where we were going. When my coordinator explained our mission, she said, "Oh, yes. We heard there was an American woman looking for old women. Well, you won't find one much older. She must be close to 115. She's the oldest one in these parts, maybe in the whole country." As we neared the house, Ljubica's grandnephew came down to welcome us and guide us to the house.

The house consists of what appeared to be one room, furnished with a daybed or couch, several wooden chairs and a wood-burning stove, next to which sat my narrator. She is a rather frail, small woman, dressed in black from head to toe. She has had the flu during the winter and is still recuperating. Her frailty does not in any way inhibit a remarkable fluidity of language, as she recalls her anguished life story. Her daughter-in-law is also in the room. After serving libations and placing bread in the oven to bake, she retires to an adjoining pantry or room from which she can oversee the bread. The two men remain outdoors during the interview. Alone now, just the two of us, her eyes firmly lock onto mine, as she takes me back through 115 years of life.

Zorka: When were you born, and where did you grow up?

Ljubica: Oh my God, *sine* [son—a most endearing and commonly used term for both sexes, reflecting the Montenegrin reverence for males], I really do not know when I was born. I know it was around *Spasovdan* [Ascension Day]. My mother died giving birth to me, and I was raised by my father's sister, my aunt. I was born far from this place, near the Monastery Piper.

I was the youngest of five children from my father's first marriage. I have one brother and five stepbrothers. Oh, no. My father did not wait long after my mother died to get married. He needed someone to take care of his children. My stepmother was alright. When there is no one better, then she was fine. Of course she beat us. There was plenty of that. But my father was a *duša* [soul]. My father was my real mother. Still, my childhood was not a happy one. Sure, as children we played and sang like all children. But we worked like everyone else. Everyone worked, but the women worked more than everyone else. They had to work inside and outside of the house. Men never do anything inside the house or with the children. Here, that is women's work. No one in this land could say anything more than life is hard. So, I do not have to tell you anymore than that.

How old were you when you married?

Oh God, *sine!* I do not know how old I was when I got married anymore than I know when I was born. I think I was around 18. Anyway, I was not yet 20 years old. My father was sick, and he said to me, "Sine, listen to me. Two men came to ask for your hand in marriage. They are from Piper [name of another tribe]. They do not have a mother and you do not, so listen to me." And he gave me to them.

I never saw my husband before I was married. My *djever* asked for my hand for his brother. I was to be married in a month's time. We needed a month so we could prepare a gift and prepare the bride. Gifts were all handmade—shirts, stockings, and some other things.

Even if I did not want to marry my husband, or found him unattractive, it did not matter. I had to do as my father said. I would not dare tell my father I did not like this man. There was no such thing as "I do not want him." That did not happen here. And the only thing that could separate them [husband and wife] was the black earth [death].

Tell me about your wedding.

On my wedding day 20 men from my husband's family came on horseback with a *barjaktar* [standard bearer] to get me. We had a lunch at my father's house and then dinner at his [the husband's] house. We were married in church [in the husband's village]. It was beautiful. There were so many people outside the church.

I was dressed in the Montenegrin national dress: a veil, a gold jacket, and silk blouse. I had to buy a gift for the bridegroom. We bought an undershirt, a vest, and a belt. We did not give money, nor cattle, nor goats. Whatever money was given as gifts at the wedding by the guests was given to me, not to my husband. We had a big *pogača* [festive, traditional round, flat bread], and on top of it people put money. The *djever* distributes the gifts after the guests have left. Oh, yes. We sang and danced the *oro*. [The *oro* (eagle) is a circle dance, emulating the dignity, grace, and posture of an eagle in flight, in the middle of which a male and a female take turns circling each other with hands outstretched, jumping in traditionally prescribed steps, similar to a fertility or mating dance performed by some tribal cultures. While in the inner circle, the couple's eyes are firmly fixed on each other. At the end of their dance, the two people kiss and return to the circle, and another couple takes their place.] And there was lots of food.

After the guests left, and it was time to go to bed, I did not sleep with my *djever*, as was the custom. I slept with my sister-in-law for two nights. I do not know how they decided that. But I did what they told me to do. Then I slept with my husband. But we had a separate room [perhaps the pantry, to which I earlier referred]. It was very difficult that first night. I was very afraid, but what could I do? He was a good man, but it was still difficult.

There were six people living in the house when I got there. My husband had no parents. There was no mother, no father, only orphans. We worked very hard. Even though I was very quiet, they all listened to me. I did not know anything, but still they listened.

I did love my husband. He was a good man. He only hit me when I deserved it. Men were very difficult with women. If he called you and you did not hear him, he would hit you. He hit you with whatever he wanted to—his hand or whatever he could grab.

Yes, my God, some men beat their wives until they could hear her *duša*. Brothers feel sorry for their sisters, but what could they do? She belongs to someone else once she is married, and they cannot help her. They try to defend her, so do brothers-in-law. Some brothers-in-law do not allow their sisters to hit their sisters-in-law. They feel sorry for them. But most times it is useless. When they want to hit you they can, and do. You have nothing to say except keep quiet. There is no sense in complaining, because there is no one to complain to. Women did not even tell their mothers they were being beaten. The only thing you can do is be quiet and do your work. Then, maybe no one will hit you. That is the way it is, not only here. You probably hear this a lot from other women.

I have to tell you that my husband never hit the children. Only his wife. Most fathers do not hit their children. He is sorry for his children. The wife does not matter. His whole family could hit her, if they want to. Here you endure, and keep quiet. You learn it is the best way.

How many children did you have ? Tell me about them.

I had three sons. Two were killed, and one is still living. My first child was a boy. My father had died, and I went to the funeral near the church. No, he did not live in this village, but in another one. I spent the night there and returned home. On my way back home with my brother-in-law and his wife, I had the baby, on the road. I was in terrible pain [she whines as she speaks]. I stooped, and the baby came out. My brother-in-law moved away from us and left us alone. My sister-in-law helped me. I walked a little, then rested, walked and rested, until we got home. My sister-in-law carried the baby.

I gave birth to two other children at home, outside. No, not on the bed. There were no beds outside. I gave birth to them on straw [in the barn]. My sister-in-law helped me with them, too. No one gave birth in the house, where people live. Never. Always outside, somewhere.

Oh, yes. There is a big difference between having a son and a daughter. Both are loved, at least by the mother. By the father also. I have to tell you that a man is very embarrassed when he has a daughter. But when it is a son, that is different. The sun shines on a son. And darkness falls on a daughter. Believe me, he [the father] does not go around bragging when it is a daughter. He does not fire a gun, nor does anyone else. Girls are not important, or not as important as boys. Ah, boys are special. They bring joy and good fortune to a house. Even mothers prefer sons. Oh, she loves her daughter, but to have a son is wealth.

You mention that you lost two sons. How did that happen?

I lost my sons right near here. They never went anywhere. Just stayed around here. During the war [World War I], they [friends] hid until they [Austrians] found them. They were killed up there on that mountain. One was 16 years old and the other 18 years old. Young boys. Too young to die. But they did. [Her sons were probably killed by artillery shells or hand grenades.]

38

I collected the remains of my sons, brought them home, and buried them. At least I know where they are. I went to the battlefield the day after the noise of guns disappeared. It was up on that hill. They did not return. I saw their brains lying on the grass. I picked them up and wrapped them in a handkerchief. Then I saw some of their bones, and other parts of their bodies. I collected them all and placed them inside of my shirt, and that is how I carried them home. I buried them myself, and no one has ever seen me cry for them. If I had cried I would have disgraced my family. No mother is ever to cry for her son or her husband. She only cries for her brother, whom she loves and honors more than any male in her life. But I cried and still cry for my sons when I am alone.

If you opened my chest you would see that my heart is lying in tears. A son is every mother's gift. Bitter is the life of a Montenegrin woman. Bitter is the life of every Montenegrin. We live with death. Our lives are blackened with pain. But it is our destiny. Pain, death, and Montenegro are the same. In this land people have to be strong, and they are strong. So we do nothing. Only we know what pain it is to bury a son. Imagine what my pain was like? I buried two at the same time. I lost two and I buried two. One 16 and the other 18. Young. So young. And I am still alive. They are gone and I am here. Fate. What else could it be?

Were women raped during the war?

There were no Turks around here. Our men chased them all out. The Turks murdered our men everywhere. There were no laws, no courts. So they [the Turks, usually Slavic converts to Islam] did whatever they wanted to do. I know many men they killed. But they did not kill the women. They had some kind of strange respect for our women. Strange!

Women were afraid of the Turks. Not one would dare go into town because the Turks had large armies there. If they felt like taking a woman for themselves, they would. They did not ask anyone. They just took, and no one could do anything except try to kill them. If only you could catch one. Whatever came to their mind, they did. My village was ruled by a Turk. He decided when we were to be married and arranged the marriages. He protected us from other Turks. But we had to work for him. Most of what we raised belonged to him, but it was the only way we could survive. It is better that way than not at all. If he wanted one of the village girls for his own, he would take her. Sometimes he would spend the first night of a girl's marriage with her, and the husband had nothing to say. You cannot get pregnant the first time. Nobody wants a Turkish child. That would be terrible! Oh, God forbid! How could you even think of that? But maybe it did happen sometimes. Sometimes you would see a child that looked like a Turk.

Of course they raped the women. God, if she became pregnant there would be lots of trouble. She would have to kill herself. She killed herself very easily. She hanged herself. If one of them had the baby, she would choke it to death. I know some women who did this. What could she do? She could not keep it, so she did the best thing for herself, the child, and her family. You cannot have a Turkish child. They are killing your people and keeping you *u robstvo* [enslaved]. Then you raise one of them? No! The best thing is to kill it. There are too many of them anyway. Anyway, you cannot get pregnant the first time. You know, most of the Turks around here are our people. Our people, who changed from our religion to theirs. They became Turks. You cannot respect people like that. They keep us *robovi* [as slaves] in our own land. Imagine! They should be ashamed of themselves. Their religion is not better than ours.

What happens to an unfaithful wife?

When a woman is unfaithful to her husband he chases her out of the house. He can not keep her. She disgraced the family, brought shame to everyone. She has to go, and that is all. What kind of man would he be if he kept her? A nothing man. Nothing! He would be worse than she. So the best thing is to get rid of her. Where does she go? Who cares where she goes. She is better off dead. Some kill themselves, some just disappear. That happens very rarely among our people. Character is very important here. Honor is everything.

I understand that women who cannot have children are not very respected. Is that true?

If a woman cannot have children, then her husband has to bring in another wife. That is all. It is important for a woman to have children. If not, that house has been *utuljena* [snuffed out]. If the first wife cannot live under those conditions, then she has to go back to her parents. That is not easy either. Parents can hardly wait to marry off their daughters. And when she comes back to them, it is very difficult. Everyone suffers. Parents are ashamed. She is ashamed. Her relatives are ashamed.

Some women who have no children will say to their husbands, "You go and get married." She gives him permission because she knows how important it is for him to have children. Besides, she feels sorry for him. If she can take it, and he does not mind having her stay, he keeps her and she waits on them. The second wife has nothing to say. And, you know, her life is easier with another woman in the house. When, God willing, a child is born, the first wife takes care of him. And everybody is happy. Happy? Nobody is happy here. I do not know anyone who has a good life. We suffer a lot. Some women do not go along with the idea of a second wife. Either way, life is difficult in Montenegro.

Even if a woman has only daughters, it is not good. If the second wife has only girls, he can bring in a third wife. I know situations where he brought in a fourth wife. He could have three or four women living in his house. No, not like the Turks. They [the Turks] just bring in women because they want more than one woman. Here, there is a good reason. He [the Montenegrin] brings in another wife only if he does not have sons. Only to have sons. Without them, what does he have? Nothing. Just nothing.

Who knows if he [the Montenegrin] sleeps with all of them. That is something we never talk about. No, I would not know about that. I never heard anything like that. But a Turk would do it. They are different. We have much honor.

What did you do when someone took ill?

There were no doctors here. What do I need a doctor for? The young ones of today are sicker with a doctor than we ever were. We were a healthy people. We did not need doctors. All we needed was food and peace. Young people today in this land have more than we ever had, yet they are not healthy or happy. We were happy and healthy. It was not our fault that we were never at peace. Outsiders never left us at peace. What did they want from us? Outside of brave men, we had nothing else. And if it were not for them we would not have survived. No matter what happens, Montenegrins can go everywhere in the world knowing they never attacked anyone or took what was not theirs. All they did was bring honor to their land. We did not even have enough food for ourselves. Doctors? God forbid! When you are sick you keep quiet at home, and maybe drink a little milk. Doctors? There were none. Nothing, not even hospitals. We just drank a little milk and sauerkraut juice. Thank God the children were healthy. Under the Turks there were no hospitals. Now we have good hospitals. I never went to a doctor or a hospital. I am as strong as an ox.

Why do you think you have lived so long?

I worked hard all my life, planting wheat, potatoes, and everything else. I worked hard and I was hungry many times. I am still here. I am the oldest in this whole area. I still last, and the others died.

I believe in God. I bless myself every night before I go to bed. I fast every Friday and Sunday. [During fasting no "fat of the land" is consumed, meaning all meats and their by-products, such as eggs, cheese, milk.] I am now fasting for Easter. [Fasts last six weeks for Easter, Christmas, and other special holy days.]

Are there differences between men and women today and in your day?

Of course. Life is easier today. Women are much smarter than men. She wants to have a family. She does not like to go to war, but she wants to work. Without a woman there is no home. But husbands do not respect that. They go to cafés, spend the money, and the family has nothing to eat. Children have to go to school. It is not like before when we had only one rag to wear, with no change of clothing. Today, they need much more, and there is much more.

Every year I go with my family to the *katun* [summer pasture], where we stay all summer. Even the children who live in the city come with us. There we take care of the animals, make cheese, and knit. Every year I walked for hours up that mountain with the rest of them. This year is different. I have had a bad flu, and I think I will have to go on horseback. [She still rides a horse and uses a wooden saddle.] I am not as strong as I used to be. Old age is old age. But I will go to the *katun*, if I am alive.

The men in my day were different, too. They did not drink, except when there was a *slava* [patron saint's day]. Today the young men drink all the time. We celebrated St. Nikolas Day. [St. Nicholas Day falls on 19 December. Orthodox Christmas is celebrated on 7 January.] We used to have many guests, men who sat around eating and drinking. They played the *gusle* [a one-stringed instrument] and sang. [*Guslars* recited lengthy, epic war poems.] We loved to listen to them. I still remember some of the songs. The young people do not care for those old ways. I am sorry for that. It is important to keep our traditions. Too much blood was spilled for them. Too much suffering. It would not be called Black Mountain if it were not black. It is steeped in blood, poverty, and death. We do not know about a good life. We never had it.

If you could have one wish, what would it be?

That my children are well and happy. Also, that I die, so I do not punish people anymore. I am a burden. Old people are.

Thank you very much.

Živa bila [May you have a long life].

MILENA

I met Milena following a visit to the Montenegrin Society of Landmark Preservation, one of whose members knew the whereabouts of an uncannily verbal centenarian woman, living on the periphery of a large town. Milena, 103 years old, does not disappoint as she effortlessly recalls the most minute details of her life. Nor is she shy. She is dismayed that there is interest in the story of an old and illiterate woman.

During our first encounter in the relatively new and large home of her son, with whom she resides, she speaks as if she has known me all her life. Proudly wearing the traditional Montenegrin dress, she, not unlike all women in this society, regardless of age, is poised and self-assured, responding clearly and succinctly to every question. One of my American colleagues said of Montenegrins, "These people must be the descendents of an ancient, aristocratic civilization." Milena's eyes, clear and attentive, reflect the aggregate wisdom of the ages—wisdom engendered by interminable suffering and struggle for survival in an unforgiving environment.

The initial interview is audiotaped in a clean, neatly furnished room, to which we are escorted by her son. Clutching a carefully folded white handkerchief and sitting comfortably upright, with crossed hands resting gently in her lap, she silently observes as I organize my interviewing paraphernalia. Not once does she appear vexed during the entire interview, and I never need to repeat a question. She is given an assignment, so to speak, and there is never any doubt she will fulfill it.

Once the interview is complete, I photograph her. Professional photographers and fashion models would envy her composure and stateliness. We then embrace; she kisses my hand and I hers, and we return to the family circle, which by now has grown considerably in number. Relatives and neighbors have come to meet the *Amerikanka* (American woman) who speaks their language and is genuinely interested in their lives.

I return several weeks later with my son, Mark, a filmmaker, to continue the interview on videotape, now outdoors, under a large, canopied tree. Neighbors sit quietly on their balconies, observing our activities from a distance. Milena is unfazed in this new setting. Once again she is dressed for the occasion, attired in her splendid traditional dress, the one in which she was married and the one in which she will be buried.

Zorka: Talk to me about your early years, when you were still living with your parents.

43

Milena: I had six sisters and three brothers. Five of my sisters and one brother died during this past war [World War II]. No one is left from my brother, except a daughter. His wife remarried, and she wanted to take her child with her, but my other brother refused to let her go. "I will raise her," he said. And that is what he did. He educated her and had her married. She has two children who finished school and served in the army. No, her mother could not take her. She had to do as she was told. The child belonged to her father's family, and that is where she stayed.

Only we children and our parents lived in the house. My grandfather was killed in the war, and my grandmother died. My mother had no one, except a brother. My father was killed in the war in Skadar [in Albania, where heavy battles were fought and numerous lives lost during the Balkan Wars]. He was a good man. He was good to his wife and children. For a week after he left for Skadar, I did nothing but cry, and I ate nothing. I cried all day long. He treated me better than he did any of the other children because I obeyed him. Whatever he told me to do, I did.

Oh God, no! He never hit my mother. She was an orphan at a young age, without a mother or father. Other mothers, *rodbina* [relatives], raised her and her brother. She got married when she was 17 years old.

How old were you when you married, and how was your marriage?

I was 21 years old when I got married, and my husband was the same age. I knew him before we were married. I am going to tell you something. I fooled my mother. I will tell you how. My father-in-law came to my uncle's house to ask if I would marry his son, and go with them. Later, my mother went to him [my uncle], and he said, "Stane, I am asking for your daughter. A good home has turned up for her here, and if you will give her to us [mother's male relatives], we can get her married." She asked me if I would marry him. "Not me, my God. I do not want him," I answered. "Really? Are you sure?" Again I told her I would not marry him. And my uncle said to her, "What did she say?" "She does not want him," my mother told him. "Well, Stane, ask her again," said my uncle. When she asked me, I said, "Mother, do whatever you want with me." See, I had already made up my mind to marry him, but I tricked her into believing that I did not want him. If I really did not want him, I guess she would force me into it, and I could not protest. Luckily, I liked him.

Did you kiss him when you saw him?

What? Kiss him? Oh, my God! Of course I never kissed him. Never! We would not even think of doing such a thing. Never! Oh God, no!

We had a very large wedding. We danced the *oro* and had lots of food and drink. I did not bring gifts to anyone. Everyone was very poor, and no one expected anything.

After everyone left, my brother-in-law, my husband's parents, and I went to bed. There was only one room in the house. I knew what to expect that first night. I knew that the husband and wife sleep together. First, I slept with my brother-in-law, as is the custom. After I fell asleep, he slipped out of the bed and went home. Then my husband came into the bed, and he did what everyone else did when they got married. Why should I be afraid? Of what? My father-in-law and mother-in-law slept in the corner of the room. They could not hear us. Besides, we waited until they were asleep.

I loved him. We loved each other. I always felt sorry for him. He worked for a daily wage. [He worked for someone else, for which he was salaried. Most people tilled their little piece of land, selling some of what they grew. Few were employed by others.]

My husband's parents were sickly people. She had one leg, and he went blind. I took care of them for many years.

I suppose you had children.

I had nine children—five daughters and three sons. No, I had eight children. My first child was born two or three years after I was married. I had him in the house. He died when he was three. He just got sick, and I took him to the hospital. The doctor said, "Take him home." There was nothing they could do for him. There was a war when that little boy was born, so no one fired a gun for him. There was no one to welcome him like they did all the other boys. I felt so sorry for my husband when that little boy died. I was especially sad because of my blind father-in-law. He was used to him. He took him out and brought him in.

Some of my children were born outside, and some near a bed or on a bed. [Like all other women, she gave birth in the barn when she gave birth indoors.] It was very difficult. I suffered for 15 days with the middle one. [I ask whether her husband helped during the birth.] What? My husband help? God forbid! He stays in the house. Someone called a friend or a sister-in-law to help me out. I never gave birth alone. Some woman was always there to help me. I raised all my children on my breasts [breast-fed them]. There was no other way.

My second child, a daughter, was born two years later. She is still living. They would not fire a gun for her, if there was a war or not. Girls were not received in the same way as boys. No man is happier than when he has a son. I was always very sorry and sad when I gave birth to a girl, and as I told you, I had five daughters. That is true in every house. Girls are not welcome in our land. Mothers also feel sad because they know how much she will suffer and how much of a *rob* [slave] she will be all her life. Always thinking of others. She will be really miserable if she does not have sons. That situation is very difficult. She could work until her *duša* oozes out, but if she does not produce sons she will not be respected or appreciated. Women without children, or women without sons, suffer more than any other women in Crna Gora. We all suffer, but her life is terrible.

Mothers of sons are as happy as any woman can be in this land. And if she has no children at all, her life is a nightmare. Everyone feels sorry for her husband, not for her. That is true. Ask anyone. He also suffers. He is angry and ashamed. He knows he has to do something about it. There is even greater pressure on him if he is an only son. If he has no sons, then his family will die out. No family can allow that to happen. That must not happen here. So he takes another wife and sends the first one home. Her parents also feel ashamed and are not happy with her or her return home. Those women spend their lives in terrible misery.

I tried to tell my husband that I cannot have any more children. I was tired and could not take it anymore. What is the sense? It does not make any difference what you say or want. It is just like talking to a donkey. Men are like donkeys, you know. I cannot think about that now. Things are no different now. Today, it is the same. Men are men, and you cannot change them. They do not listen. He does not have to do all the work and take care of them [the children]. I really do not care. It is all over for me.

You said the loss of your little boy was very difficult. Was it especially so because he was a son rather than a daughter?

When my son died I told you how sad everyone was. But I never cried for him in public. That was not allowed. No mother is allowed to cry for her son. In your greatest pain, you could not cry. It was a sign of weakness if you did. I would go under the house to cry. My heart would be breaking, but I had to be very careful so that no one would hear me. I would wipe my tears and my face before anyone could see me. I had to go around as if I did not bury a son. Do you know how hard that is? I hope you never know. May your son live long and bring you happiness. Sons are happiness. Losing a daughter is sad, but not as sad as losing a son. That is the worst.

My husband died when he was 60 years old. I did not cry for him either. Oh God! If they saw me cry, they would laugh at me. I really never cried for him, even when I was alone. The loss of a son is the most painful thing in the world, and for him I always cry. But, as I told you, I will never cry for him in public.

The loss of a brother is worse than any loss in this country. A sister loves a brother more than anyone else in the world. You can imagine what happens when she loses him. Oh God! It is so painful. My heart aches when I think of my brother. There is nothing a sister will not do for her brother. She will kill for him if she has to. She will gladly give her life for him. Unless you have lost a brother you do not what that pain is like. I cannot explain to you why we feel that way, but we do. From very early, a girl is taught to love her brother, and she does. Ask any woman in this land about that and she will tell you. Of course I scratched my face at my brother's funeral. You would, too. I wished a thousand times I had died instead of him. I wished I was dead. My face was all full of blood. Can you imagine how my mother felt, the one who raised him? Every one around her was crying, screaming, and beating themselves, and she could not even shed a tear. Our people watch for that. If she cried, people would talk about it forever.

My poor father was killed in the war at Skadar. When I heard that he was dead, I threw my son on the stairs. My mother said, "Milena, Why did you throw him?" But I did not even know where I was at the time. We have had so much death in our land, yet we never get accustomed to it. When someone goes to war, you almost have to expect that he will never come back. Yet when it happens it is horrible. Unbearable!

Even men mourn and cry at the cemetery. We cried over my father's clothing. My mother always kept it in sight to remind us of our brave father. Tears and pain. Pain and tears. That is Crna Gora!

Was there much hunger during wars?

There was a lot of hunger around here. During the time of the Austrians [1878–1918] I worked in the fields, and sometimes I did not eat for three months. Well, I ate grass and nettles. I picked the nettles out of holes, cut them up, and cooked them without salt. No one in my family died of hunger, but we came close.

What happens to an unfaithful wife, or to a pregnant unmarried girl?

One of my daughters had a baby out of wedlock. After a while she married. Today she lives with her son, whom she had married [his mother arranged his marriage]. He goes to work, so does his wife.

Of course I did the honorable thing; I threw her out of the house. She could never stay here after she disgraced us all. You know how bad that is in this country? It is one of the worst things that could happen to a family. We are an honorable people. We may be poor, but we have *obraz*. [*Obraz*, which means "cheek," is like the Japanese concept of "face," perhaps one of the most widely used expressions in Montenegro, which is not surprising in a society obsessed with honor. A "white" *obraz* enables one to meet the public and look them in the eye, unlike a "black" *obraz,* which signifies shame. This was a common word in my own home.]

Everyone here lives that way, and then, when something like this happens, it is horrible. My daughter went away and lived in the home of some woman, and that is where she gave birth. She then got married and became a widow. She never got anything from the first one [the father of her child], but the second one [her husband] left her his house. She sold it and bought a house for her son. You see, even here, where a good reputation is what is most important, things go on that are not supposed to.

An unfaithful wife has a miserable life. Some husbands keep it quiet, but her life is worthless. He could beat her as much as he wants, and she has to take it. Some men send her back to her parents, where her life is not any better. She could be beaten there, too, and treated with disrespect. Either way her life is over, even if she stays alive. This is no place for someone like that.

How many wars do you remember? That is, how many wars did you live through?

The first war I remember was the Turkish War. I also remember the Austrian War. My father was in the war in Skadar. All the men went there; only women and children stayed behind. Even some old men went. We [women and children] had to do all the work, inside and out, and provide food for our children. But that was nothing new to us. We worked if there was a war or not. Whatever we could gather from the land we took to Cetinje [then the capital of Montenegro] and sold it for bread.

I also went to Skadar to take food to my father. That was very far away, in Albania. We [women, often as many as 20, traveled in groups] walked and rested, then walked some more. There were no roads. We took him bread, potatoes, meat, and stockings. When we got to some villages near Skadar, we saw our army. The ones we first saw were not wounded, but they were dirty, unwashed. Who knows when they last washed. Why were they unwashed? Who is there to wash them? There were not any women there. We were all at home. Men are fighters. Who would protect us? Everything else has to be taken care of for them. That is what women are for.

I will tell you a story about my brother. Two women in my family were kidnapped by Turks when they were taking food to their men in Albania. My brother swore that he would avenge them. He decided that he would find the men and cut off their noses. No *Crnogorac* [Montenegrin male] was taking heads then. But he could not find the men. One day he came across a Turk, but could not cut off his nose because he did not have a knife on him. So he did what he could, he bit off the Turk's nose. That is the way it was then. I told you before that nothing is easy in this country. Everybody suffered.

Were women raped during wars?

No. I never heard of any woman being raped, even by the Turks, who would do something like that if they could. We protected ourselves, and our men protected us. Men protect women in this country.

One time, when we were up in the *katun* [summer pasture] when I was young, a man ran after me. I told my father, and he ran after him with a scythe. If he caught him, he would have killed him. I never gave him any reason to chase me. If we did not behave properly and modestly, we would ruin not only our reputation but also that of our families. Women knew how to behave then. Three of my sisters got married in the same year. My family has a good name.

How do children take care of their parents today?

Today it is better to have one of your children die than your husband. Mothers are not looked after now the way they were at one time. I took good care of my mother-in-law. Before she died, she said to my husband, "Son, are you there?" "Yes, I am." She continued, "Listen to what I have to say." "What?" he said. "Take a piece of my clothing for Milena, because I caused her a lot of trouble," she said. She was so weak she could not get up to give it to him. She was bedridden and near death.

Today's children do not do that. They do not take care of their parents. In the old days, three- and four-year-old children tended to the goats. Today's children are taken care of. They are educated. Today's children are not for work. They are for school. No, that is not good. Children should listen to their parents. No parent wishes his child ill. They would drown themselves for their children. But I must tell you, this woman [her grandson's wife] is good to me. I am happy here. As long as they are alive [her children and grandchildren and their families], I am happy.

What would you wish for if I could grant you a wish?

I wish to see my sister-in-law's granddaughter have a baby, even if it is a girl. The next one will be a boy. I also wish to die, so I remove myself and do not bother them. I do not think I bother them, but still I feel as if I am more work for them.

Thank you for talking to me about your life.

Srečna i zdrava bila [May you be fortunate and healthy].

PETRANA

To reach 103-year-old Petrana from the main artery proved quite difficult. Invariably, my driver inquired in advance as to our destination. Initially I presumed that he needed time to plan the most expeditious route, which was partly the case. More important, he had to decide which automobile would best handle the terrain. When our destination took us beyond the primary and secondary roads to where there were no roads, merely horse-cart paths, he left behind the Mercedes, the Peugot, the Russian Lada, and the large Fiat. The automobile of choice was a Yugo. This four-cylinder marvel went where no other would dare to tread: through tall grasses and bushes, often requiring removal of large branches before we could proceed; through foot-deep mud; over kilometers of rocks; up and down steep hills. Having become accustomed to large Western vehicles, the sight of the Yugo was at first disquieting, but not for long. It proved to be a trouper.

No sooner did we park the car than our host, Petrana's son, an older, tall, slightly bent man with a weather-beaten face and blue eyes, came around the bend to greet us and to lead us to her. His house sits in the middle of a large expanse of land, surrounded by snow-peaked mountains, overlooking a valley of green, rolling hills. Eagles flew overhead in this bucolic setting on a day as clear as any I have ever witnessed. Standing in the midst of such tranquility, my only thoughts were of harmony and brotherhood. Petrana's story would return me to the dark side of nature. Like most of Crna Gora, this seeming Shangri-la has been soaked in human blood and hatred. After exchanging a few words at the front entrance with her daughter-in-law, a tall, thin, and energetic woman with a tired-looking but fine-featured face, we were ushered into the house.

Petrana, who has broken her hip and is unable to arise, sits on a couch, next to a wood-burning stove. I approach her, kissing her and offering my gift of green coffee. The couch is covered with a *čilim* (handmade rug), above which hangs a framed photograph of Petrana and her husband, both young and in traditional Montenegrin dress. Today she is wearing that same dress. It is obvious that she is quite tall, at least 5'10". Despite her broken hip, which causes her considerable distress, she sits upright and appears alert. Several minutes later, everyone, except Petrana and I, vacates the room. Following the interview, we all came together to enjoy the homemade cheeses (new and aged), yogurt, freshly baked bread, and *pršuta* (thinly sliced smoked ham) and, of course, *šlivovica* (plum brandy).

The interview was for me one of the most soul wrenching. I thought that by this time I had become somewhat stoic, but I was wrong.

Zorka: Tell me about your life with your parents.

Petrana: Today, on St. George's Day [6 May], I am 103 years old. I have lived many years, and I was always poor. I was born here in the mountains. I have nothing now, nobody. They all died. When I was young I had many. I had two uncles, mother and father—I had all of that. Now, I have no one from my *rod* [birth family]. I also had seven or eight brothers. Yes, seven or eight brothers and three sisters. I was the oldest in the family. I even went to Skadar during the Balkan Wars.

What can I talk to you about, *jadna* [poor thing—frequently used as a term of endearment]? I cannot say anything except that my life was hard. I suffered when I was little, I suffered when I grew up. Oh, when I think of what I lived through! The best thing is to forget about it. But when you ask me, I have to tell you. There is nothing I can say that is good. My uncles were good. They were my father's brothers. My father? Like every other father. He hardly ever spoke to me, unless he wanted me to get him something. Now that you ask me, I cannot even remember if he ever said a word to me. He did not speak to my mother either. None of the men spoke much to the women. They talked to one another. During supper? We never sat together. We did not eat with the men. The men sat and ate by themselves, while the women were always doing something. Most of them never sat down, even to eat. Now you know how much we suffered, and how hard it is here.

We were many in the house—my uncles, two aunts, father and mother, and my 10 or 11 brothers and sisters. But I am the healthiest, and here I am. I have never had a headache. We lived in three rooms. Three rooms; most lived in one room. My mother, *jadna,* died. She was in the Turkish war [Montenegrins were perpetually at war with the Montenegrin converts to Islam; Petrana's mother lived through perhaps one of the more intense battles] and suffered a lot. We worked very hard. We had 200 sheep, 20 cows, and oh, how hard I worked! Some children went to school, but I was never in school. It was not our custom for girls to go to school. Even the boys went for only a few years. Now everybody goes to school.

How did you meet your husband?

I was 20 years old when I got married. After that I went to Skadar. Someone just came and asked for my hand in marriage. My God, they were big men. [She probably meant exceptionally tall and physically well developed men. It is not uncommon to see men over 6'7" tall.] They came from far away, across that *greda* [divide], those large rocks. Across the *greda*. See my husband before I married him? No! No! Believe me. I never saw him. His family and others came to ask for me. My uncle did not want to give me to them. But when your father promises you to someone you have to go. A man's word is respected, and when he gives it, he gives it. His word is his honor. My father said to them, "I never lied in my life. I give her to you." My husband was 22 years old, so he was not much older than me. And here I am today, St. George's Day, and I am 103 years old!

What kind of a wedding did you have?

They [the husband's family] came to get me, and they took me to their house, where I was married. My parents treated them very well when they came. They prepared a nice meal, and the men who came to get me ate. Then they took me away. I had a big wedding, with a lot of barbecued meat and other things. There was music, and I sang and danced. I weighed 93 kilos [about 200 lbs.]. I was a big woman, and here I am today—103 years old on St. George's Day!

I spent the first night of my married life in bed with my two brothers-in-law. In the same bed, of course. They were married, so their wives slept with us, too. All in the same bed. And then, the second night I slept with my husband for the first time. We did not sleep in the same room with the others. We had a separate room. Did we kiss a lot? What a question! A joke! [You must be kidding!] He never said a nasty word to me. He never said, "*Crne ti oči*" [May you never see daylight]. He never hit me either. God forbid!

Did you have many children?

I had 14 children; 14, my God! The first one was born a year and a half after I was married. It was a son. My husband and all the villagers fired their guns and celebrated. I was happy, too. But, my God, my two oldest died. The oldest one was 12 years old when he died. He "flew" out of school [came home from school suddenly]. Oh, if I only knew from what he died, he would not have died. I would not let him die. He died from *žutica* [yellow jaundice—infectious hepatitis]. My second son died from the same thing when he was four years old. Many people died from that sickness. We had no doctors. We did not even know what it was. It just came and killed so many, even my two sons. Ah, God! My third son was also very sick, and they [the village women] told me to take him to water where there are fish and to keep pushing him into it. And look! Today I have four or five grand-sons from him.

I also buried a daughter when she was little. I do not know from what she died. I nursed them all. And here I am, 103 years old. Today is my birthday; 103 years! But she [the daughter] died. There is no one to tell us what kind of sickness people died from. All of a sudden they get sick and die. That is how it happened with my daughter. I cannot remember how old she was, but I know that she was little—little.

After the first two sons I had a daughter. My husband liked her very much. Of course he did not fire his gun, nor did anyone else. We only do that when a son is born. No one would fire a gun for a girl. Those were the old days. That is the way it was in those times. Sons are special. So they fire guns for them. Not for girls.

Were your children born in a hospital?

Have a baby in a hospital? What hospital? We had no hospitals, not even doctors. Hospital? No doctor. No woman. I did it all by myself. I had them in the house and out there [pointing outside of the house]. Where would I have them if not in the house? I just go into the house, and in that corner over there I gave birth, with no one's help. I did not go to the mountains with them [the summer pasture] over there. Oh, God! So many children. [She keeps sighing and nodding her head, and repeating over and over, "14 children, 14 children, so many children, a lot of children. Oh, God!"] Today I have six daughters, four sons, five grandchildren, and others [great-grand-children].

What happened to wives who were unfaithful or to girls who had children out of wedlock?

I never heard of an unmarried girl having a baby. That never happened in my time. Today it happens every hour. Now they are freer. They do not listen to their parents. They do whatever they want. We could never do that.

If a wife cheated on her husband, she was in a lot of trouble. He could chase her out of the house. Once that happens, the only place she could go is back to her parents. That would not be easy for her either. They married her as an honorable girl from a good family, and now she brings disgrace to her *rod* and her *dom* [to both families]. Do you see what she did? That never happens here. Maybe it does, but not to anyone I know. Imagine, she will never see her children again, just because she could not control herself. Never see her children. Never!

Supposing a woman cannot have children. What happens to her?

What can her husband do? What can he do? She cannot, she cannot. No, he does not leave her. Look here! I have a daughter-in-law who has no children, and here she is. It is very difficult among *Crnogorci* [Montenegrins] when there are no children, especially if there are no sons. So it was hard for my son and his wife. It was hard for all of us. But it is too late now. Too late [she sighs]. It is difficult. Difficult. [Her tormented expression reveals the agony she has endured in a society in which the bearing and raising of children is an all-consuming raison d'être.]

What was it like when you went to Skadar?

I went to Skadar during the Turkish war. Oh, *jadna ja* [poor me]! At first, they did not let my father go to his son in Skadar. After a while, he went, too. So I went there on foot [about a six-day walk from where she lived]. How else? How would I get there? That is the only way for all of us, even soldiers. We went everywhere on foot. We do not know any other way. Do you hear me? You hear? I was about 20 years old when I went to Skadar. My two uncles, my father, a nephew, and Vlado [her brother, the only person she calls by name during the entire interview]. Oh God, I carried so many things to them, meat, cheese, and other things.

Later, they would not let me go. My family would not let me. I had to work in the fields and light the fire [for cooking and warmth].

After Skadar was taken [by the Albanians], the army came back. I went with them and about 20 women to Mojkovac [a town where vicious battles were fought against the Turks in August 1911]. We came near Pljevlje, and then to Metak, where we met the army—the *Švabe* [Austrians]. They did not bother us, but there were three or four border guards who had escaped and drowned in the Drina [river]. Those were our men running away from the *Švabe*. My uncle also ran with them, and when he returned the *Švabe* captured him and put him in prison. Oh, *joj* [Woe is me]! My father sent me home because I had to cut hay. There were no men around. They were all taken as prisoners. All captured!

You seem to have been especially fond of your brother Vlado.

Oh God, my Vlado died in an unfair way. He was so handsome, my God. The peasants betrayed him. They betrayed him to the *Švabe*, and the *Švabe* killed him. They wanted him to tell them something. I went up there to where they had him. They wanted to kill me—to kill me. Oh God, when I saw him, it was so pitiful! He had no hands [pointing to an area between

55

the elbow and wrist]. He had no hands! No hands! [At this point she sobs uncontrollably for her brother, who died more than 75 years ago. When she is speaking of the deaths of her children and other family members, she sits resigned, never shedding a tear.]

Do you hear me? My brother had no hands! No hands! He held on to a rock while they cut them off. Up to here—his hands, up to here. No, no, not with guns! He kept circling around the rock, and they forced him to keep his hands on the rock. As he circled, they kept beating him with the butts of their rifles until they broke every bone, and he kept running around the rock. He was no more guilty than I was, yet they, the *seljaci* [the villagers or peasants; the two names were interchangeable in Montenegro, where all men are recognized as equals] handed him over to them. I was all alone, and when they cut off his hands I went up to him. The *Švabe* did not try to stop me. I picked him up, put him up over my shoulders, and carried him home.

I carried him so that I could bury him. I could see he was going to die. I did not cry or wail. Oh God, I was strong! And I carried and carried, never crying nor wailing. I carried him home by myself, over my shoulders. My mother had gone into the town with my aunt, where she asked someone, "Do you know anything about him? He was killed? How was he killed?" He said, "Out of a gun." She was very brave and strong-hearted, and said, "That is good. As long as they did not break his bones with a chair." [It was considered an honor for a warrior to die by a bullet.] When she came back from town—my poor mother, when she saw him, when she saw him! She sat next to him and said, "*Sine, srečne ti rane*" [Son, may your wounds be fortunate; *Srečne ti rane* is also a metaphor, wishing him a speedy recovery from his wound so he can go into battle again]. He looked up at her, enough to say to his mother, "*Zdrava bila, Majko*" [May you be healthy, Mother], and he let go of his soul. "*Zdrava bila, Majko*," and he never said another word.

We dug him a grave. [She illustrates how they dug the grave with their hands.] My mother and aunt and I did it. His mother dressed him in traditional Montenegrin attire. Three *Švabe* came along and saw what we were doing, saw us in this way. Then my mother took a large cloth, and two of the *Švabe* gave their guns to the third one. They took the cloth from my mother, and they wrapped him up in it. We did not have a coffin. We buried him just like that, in his Montenegrin clothing, wrapped in a cloth. My mother, my aunt, and I, the three of us, carried him to his grave. I carried him in the front, and they carried him in the back. When we got him to the grave, the *Švabe* helped us push him in, pushing the cloth around him into the grave. And I kept pushing him into the grave, without a coffin. Did you hear? Without a coffin! Oh God, oh God [she sobs]! I keep thinking back on that. Oh God! Now I have no one. I buried them all. Sickness came and took them.

Did you cry for your husband when he died?

Cry for my husband? Why? I had my children to take care of. I had no time for anything else. I took care of them. Why should I cry? He was born, so he had to die. *Laka mu crna zemlja* [May the black earth lie lightly on him]. Why should I cry for him? Yes, it is true. I mourn more for my brothers than for anyone else. And I have buried so many, even my children. I grieve day and night for my brothers. They [her family and the villagers] make fun of me. I know all that has passed, but it does not go away. It will never go away. It hurts, hurts. Oh God, it hurts, hurts. It hurts too much. Too much!

Was there any hunger here?

Oh God, so many died over there from hunger! Over there. What the devil is the name? [She cannot remember the place.] They had nothing to eat, and so they died—so many of them, you could hardly count them. Many were killed, and others just died. The *Švabe* killed my brother. May the devil devour them. The devil devour them!

Were any women raped in your time?

The *Švabe* rape women? Oh, my God, they were better than our men. Neither did our men rape the women. But I have to tell you that the *Švabe* never bothered us until our peasants betrayed us. We suffered more because of our own people than we did from the *Švabe*. I am telling you that is the way it was.

What is the difference between the women of today and the women in your day?

Oh, the older women were much better. Today women walk on their toes [high heels—implying that modern women are not prepared to work, as are the older women]. They do not even raise their own children. They go to work and leave the children for others to raise. We had to work, and work hard in the fields and in the house. Still, we had to take care of our children. Today they have one child, and they cannot take care of it. That is why women were better before. Do you understand? Women have it much easier today, but they are not the kinds of mothers we were. We cared for our children all the time. We never had any time for ourselves. Never! All of our time was spent taking care of everybody in the house. Nobody helped us. You had your children, and you raised them yourself. That is the way it was.

If you were given one wish, what would it be?

I want nothing. I just want my sons to be healthy, and my daughters-in-law. My time is finished. They are beginning, just beginning. I would rather die. I need to rest. I am going into the next life, and I never had a headache or saw a doctor. I have lived too long. I just curse myself because I continue to live. I have no natal family, just one grandson from my brother. He lives over there in Titograd. Why should I live deaf, blind, without a leg [with a broken hip]? I would rather die. If I could only run to the place where my sons and husband are, and my brothers. My brothers, brothers! Oh, God! My brothers!

Hvala najlepša [Thank you kindly].

Pomaga ti Bog [May God help you].

PART 2

The Honeymoon Must Wait

On a mother's tombstone may be written in large letters:

This Clump of Dirt Covers the Most Brilliant Teacher of Love
Before This Burial Mound All Who Are Grieving Should Humble Themselves
For the Last Time, from the Grave, She Can Say Only, "You Are Right,
I Owe Nothing to Anyone"
Here Lies Sophocles' Epic and Homer's Tragedy
Every Grave Is Too Small for a Mother
—Son's eulogy at mother's grave, from Todor Baković's Depresivni
Optimizam Crnogoraca

One of the most enigmatic traditions in Montenegro concerning marriage rituals takes place on the wedding night. In this land, consummation does not take place on that night or, in some cases, for several months following the wedding. Though it may surprise many, there is a logical reason for such a practice. Marriages are arranged. Bride and groom come to the union as strangers, frequently from distant villages. Strangers—her father-in-law and brothers-in-law—escort her from the home of her parents to a strange village, into a strange home, where she will marry a stranger. One can only speculate as to the amount of fear and trepidation she experiences.

The patriarchy, far from being indifferent to her anxieties, provides a mechanism that allows for a less traumatic transition into her new environment. Her new home, not unlike the home from which she came, consists of one room in which reside an average of 8 to 10 children and adults—her new family. People know it will take time for her to adjust to a new setting, to feel as secure and loved as any member of the family. It is equally important for her family to know that their daughter is respected and protected. Through the union of their children, the two families have formed close ties. Any disrespect shown toward her reflects disrespect for her family.

Recognizing how difficult it is at best for an innocent young woman to sleep with her husband for the first time—a man she has just met—tradition dictates that she spend the first night with her brother-in-law, both fully clothed. The oldest woman in the home may then insist that the bride sleep with her or with some other woman in the family for an additional period of time. To my knowledge, there is no documented explanation for the extension. When asked, the women merely say, "That is the way it was."

Because honor is firmly inculcated in every member of Montenegrin society, there is never any fear of the brother-in-law taking advantage of his brother's wife. Mere sexual innuendo on his part is sufficient grounds for taking his life—something of a fail-safe system. It is incumbent upon his father or brother to fulfill that task, thus restoring honor to the family. Not doing so could incite the bride's family to initiate a blood vendetta.

Obviously, the bride does not feel relaxed in her new home overnight, or perhaps for years. Nevertheless, even at this early stage of married life, she has been assured that no harm will come to her, that she is as secure with her new family as she was with her birth family. Within the structure of a traditional patriarchy, Montenegro has provided the framework for a moral and ethical society in which every member is integral to the whole.

JELENA

One-hundred-and-two-year-old Jelena lives with her grandson and his family in a small house, nestled in a tranquil valley among snow-capped mountains in a skier's paradise. Five or six horses run freely across the fields, one leading the others. The driver is ever-watchful for snowslides and mudslides. We hear that a week or so before our arrival, a young man, walking home from town, was killed in a snowslide. So dangerous are the roads that we are taken in a police jeep to Jelena's home. From where we park, there is a considerable walk to her home, down a long, winding path. So narrow is the path that we walk in single file.

There is never any lack of conversation, either in the jeep or during the walk. In this country one's adrenalin is forever being regenerated, if not by the exhilarating natural beauty, stark and foreboding in places, then certainly by the people and their loquaciousness. Should they intuit that someone is interested in them, their lives, and especially their history, they delight in sharing every detail. It is so on this trip, as it is on all the others.

Long before we gain sight of the house, a male member of the family, no doubt hearing our voices, welcomes us and leads us to our destination. And there they are, in what serves as the living room and kitchen. Because friends and neighbors are also there to greet us, it is almost impossible to ascertain how many live in the house. Visiting each house is truly a social event. Jelena sits among the many. It is not difficult to discern who I came to interview. Not only is she the oldest, but she is also the only one wearing traditional Montenegrin dress. I present her with my gift of coffee, after kissing her three times. She is also the one receiving the most attention from all who are there. And she loves it. This is unquestionably one of the highlights of her life—a day centering on a century-old woman who has received little attention, although her role has been of irrefutable significance—duly attested to by all. She participates in the conversation only when specifically addressed, responding succinctly and confidently.

Following the libations, Jelena and I are escorted to a downstairs room that can be reached only from outside of the house. (Without exception, men lead us to where the interviews take place.) I assist her as we walk, although she could have done perfectly well without me. Once the others have gone, it does not take long for the interview to begin. She observes my every movement as I set up the recording equipment, smiling each time I meet her glance. I endeavor to be as professional as possible, though more often than not I find myself conversing with these women as I would with endearing friends. Perhaps that is why I am successful with my interviews. Jelena, like so many of the other women, kisses my hands as we talk—so delighted is she that it is because of her that I am here. After the interview is complete and the photograph taken, we warmly embrace, as she strokes my hair and face. It is not easy to contain my emotions.

Zorka: Talk to me about your early years, before you were married.

Jelena: I never went to school. There were no schools then, hardly any-where—certainly not in this village. Not only was there not a school here, but there were also never any roads here. They built roads after the war [World War II]. Anyway, we had no cars. We walked everywhere. Most of us never left the village.

I never dated any men. God, no! I did not want to because something always stopped me from doing so. [Hers was an interesting response, since dating was inconceivable in her day.] There was too much work to be done around the house. That was most important. Too many people depended on us. There were many of us. I had parents and brothers and sisters. They all had to be taken care of, so we all had to work as soon as we could. Even children worked, especially girls. Girls always worked hard.

How did you meet your husband?

I was old when I got married—22 years old. I knew my husband because he lived around 30 meters from my house. He was three years younger. No one really cared if he was younger or older. I liked him.

Did you kiss him before or after you became engaged?

What? What? God forbid! I never kissed him! I give you my word. It was the custom. There was no love. When they [the husband's family] asked for a girl's hand in marriage, they never asked her if she wanted to get married at all. Parents decided that, and you had to respect their wishes. All that parents want to know is if she comes from a good family. Family reputation is all that matters. When the time comes for both the boy and girl [when they are of marriageable age], others make the arrangements. Not even do they ask the young man if he wants her or not. Liking each other did not matter. Parents never asked that question. The young man's family decides that it is time for him to get married, so they ask around to see where there is an available girl, and that is it.

You know, my parents did ask me if I wanted him, and I guess I could have refused him, but I did not. I could not refuse him. My God, after my father, brother, and mother gave me to him! I had to obey them. To continue to obey, work, care for, stack hay and anything else that needed to be done. We are never told what to do. We know what has to be done, and we do it, without complaining, arguing, or, God forbid, refusing to do it. We just keep quiet and do what we are supposed to do.

And your wedding? What was that like?

Six men from my husband's family arrived on horseback, and they stayed at my parents' house, where my family had prepared a nice meal. After several hours, they took me to my husband's home. I wore the traditional Montenegrin dress, all embroidered in gold. I was beautifully dressed. My brother bought me everything. For a wedding gift I gave my mother-in-law a shirt [or blouse], which I had made myself. There was no father-in-law. He was dead. I did have a brother-in-law, but he was forced into the army in Hungary, where he died. They [the family] gave him everything they had, and he sold it for tobacco. His body was never returned. So, only my husband, his mother, and sister lived in the house. My wedding lasted two days. There was no music because we were always at war. But they played the *gusle* [an ancient one-stringed instrument], and everyone danced the *oro,* including me.

A month passed before I slept with my husband. I slept with my sister-in-law, and my husband slept with his mother in the other bed. That was the custom. When they [the husband's family] brought the bride home and she slept with her husband immediately, she would be disgraced. Why would she be disgraced? Well, because they will say she cannot wait to go to bed with him. Oh, God! That would be a terrible disgrace! There were very strict customs, and you had to do whatever they said. So his family decides when you sleep with your husband. The women do that. Yes, I did it too. I cannot remember how it happened.

After a month passed, my sister-in-law said to me, "I do not want to sleep with you anymore." After that, I slept with my husband, and my sister-in-law and mother-in-law slept together in the other bed, all in the same room. I was not frightened when I first slept with my husband. It was dark, and no one could see anything. It was a large room, like a barrack. Later on the army burned it down.

You must have lived through many wars.

I remember four wars, Turkish, German, Austrian, and Bulgarian. We were always hungry and thirsty. We were always running away from an army, and when they left, we went home. That is the way we lived most of my life. My husband was home the whole time. He was never in the army, except for a short time. I remember when the *Švabe* came here. I was in a little shanty, lying down with my children. Two soldiers came in and went right for the mattresses, looking for something. They found some bread I had hidden under them. They took the bread, and I said, "Why did you take my bread? My children will die." They said, "Shut up, old lady!" They took the bread and left. There was also a little lard, but they only took the bread. The German army always behaved honorably when they were not attacked. When they were attacked, they took whoever they came across—women, children, even animals. I do not know what they did with them. They took them away, and we never saw them again. Their soldiers never raped the women. They were very honorable.

Did you have many children?

I had nine children—two sons and seven daughters. My first child, a daughter, was born a year and a half after I was married. My husband was not too upset because I had a girl. No one was angry. But when a son is born they fire guns. But times were difficult, so there was little celebration even when a son was born. Those were bad times. Sons are always special, especially in Crna Gora.

I had all my children at home. We never went to a hospital to have a baby. There was not even a hospital around here. All the women had their babies at home. No doctors either. I went into a corner of the room, where I stayed until the baby came. Some neighbor or relative would help by bathing the child and wrapping it up. Sometimes I gave birth lying down, at others I would stoop. What could we do? We did the best we could. No, not many children died when they were born. Even if we are poor, we are a very healthy people.

Are all your children living?

I buried four children. Three died when they were very young. One of them was three or four years old. I even buried a grown daughter. She was 40 years old, married with no children. She just became ill, went to the hospital, and died. Just like that.

My husband died about 30 years ago. I did not mourn for him much. Why should I mourn for him? He died . . . he died. What could I have done? I did not even cry for him; not even for the children, let alone him. Some women carried on when someone died. They even scratched their faces, but not me.

Did you remarry?

I never wanted to remarry after my husband died. [I suspect her husband died much earlier than she recalls. She speaks of leaving her children behind, should she have remarried.] I could not leave my children behind. You know, I could never take the children with me if I remarried. The children always stay in the family and the house where they were born. When a woman remarries she goes alone with her new husband. The children stay where they are. She knows that, but she leaves anyway. I guess her husband is more important than her children. Some women I know did leave their children and went away to another village with their new husband. Sometimes, she never sees her children after that. Never! Never! There are all kinds of mothers in this world. I am one of those who could never leave her children to go with a man. Never!

What happened to an unfaithful wife?

Women were rarely unfaithful here. She would not dare be unfaithful. If she were, she would not fare too well. He [the husband] could kill her, or beat her every day. That happened. Sometimes, he would first kill his wife, and then leave. No one knows where he went or whether he is alive or dead. That is a terrible disgrace here, and everybody knows it, so it does not happen often. A good woman knows that. The children stay behind and are raised by their aunt, their father's sister, or whoever is living in the house. When they [the children] got older, they got married.

Did women socialize with one another very much?

Women always got together with other women for talk and coffee. The older women even drank [alcohol]. Mothers-in-law mostly. [Older women, of whom most are widowed, enjoy considerably greater freedom than do younger women. Some drink and smoke, enjoy listening to and telling jokes of a sexual nature, even use obscene language, for which a younger woman would be severely ostracized and punished.] We younger women just worked, and worked hard. There was no coffee and talk for us. Oh, no, not for us.

Husbands and wives used to argue and fight a lot. We never did, nor did my husband ever hit me. The young people of today have everything, so there is no need to fight. Poor people fight. Today, young women have everything they need in the house. We never had anything. When you are poor, there are a lot of arguments. Even children fight when they are poor. No one is happy. How can you be happy when you have nothing? Nobody has anything. I do not think most people would fight if they had what they need. In my time, most people had barely enough to survive, and we had lots of children. You had nothing to give your children. You were glad when you could feed them. It is never easy in a poor land. And we were poor— as poor as they come. Right now we have everything. You should have seen how it was when I was young. You would not believe it.

With all of the poverty and the sadness in your life, why do you think you have lived to this age?

Fate. What else could it be? The way I lived I should have died years ago, like my daughter did. But it was not my destiny. Now, I am tired. I have been here long enough. It is time to go. But it looks like it is not my time, even if I wish it. Fate. My fate. I cannot explain it to you because I do not know myself. I did not die, and that is all. My fate.

Thank you very much.

Zdrava bila [May you be healthy].

VIDOSAVA

Vidosava lives alone in a small village. Her family is scattered around the country in large cities. Her son, hearing about my research, contacted me. His first words were, "My mother is more than 100 years old, uncannily verbal, with a remarkable memory. I think you would like to interview her. She could tell you a great deal about what life was like when she was young. She lived the way Montenegrins lived for centuries before her time. Things did not change that fast around here. I will take you to her in my car."

On our way to the interview my coordinator fills me in with some of the history of the region. Montenegrins are born social scientists, right down to the illiterate peasant, the cab driver, and the centenarian woman. If it is the history of Montenegro that someone wants to know about, the man in the street—a natural historian and ethnographer—is a good resource. He will happily oblige. After all, he grows up repeatedly hearing about and reliving the past. That is what men did and continue to do. Dates and details of glorious battles, won and lost, slip off their tongues in as fluid a language as one has ever heard.

Vidosava is 103 years old. Though illiterate, she recites hundreds of lines of epic war poetry, stopping only to explain the characters and interpret their actions for her American visitors. She is especially animated in the presence of my son, who videotapes one of the interviews. Since she doubts that I could know Montenegro's history well, she feels it incumbent upon herself to familiarize him with his ancestral past, much as she did with her own children. My first encounter with Vidosava is in a field behind her house, where, pitchfork in hand, she is stacking hay—a startling sight, to be sure. A tall, slender woman dressed in black, she exudes the energy of a considerably younger person, of one never having known deprivation in any form. Yet, as she describes it, her life was nothing but tribulation. Walking back to the house, we chat as family, without formality or apprehension. Her son serves coffee on the terrace, after which we are led into the house.

I interview her in a fairly cold, dimly lit room. Sitting in a comfortable chair, calm and confident, she recounts her distant past as if having just recently lived it. The only question she declines to answer is one about her sexual life. Indeed, I take a risk by asking it. Maintaining her composure, she says, "Do not ask me that. Ask me something else." What she did reveal follows.

Zorka: Tell me about your life before you were married.

Vidosava: Before I was married I lived with my parents, a brother and four sisters. They are all dead now. We, like everyone else, did not have much. Still, we were not too poor. I tended sheep and sewed on a sewing machine. We were one of the few who had one. My brother was in America. He sent me money to buy it. I made everything on that sewing machine. Underwear for everyone, plus dresses and skirts. We also went to the *katun,* all of us, except my brother who was in America. He was killed during World War I in France, and we never found him. He was a soldier in the American army. He got married here, left for America and never came back. He made a lot of money. He was from my father's first marriage. My father also had a daughter. His wife died, but I do not know what from.

My mother then married him, even if he was a widower with children. She married him because he was very good looking. He went to her village, saw her, and she married him. She came into a house with children. You can imagine the work she had. Then she had her own children, which meant even more work. Like everyone else, she had to get permission from her father to marry him. No woman married without permission from her family. Marrying a widower was not too common in those days. Today it is no problem. They do everything today.

I never fell in love when I was young, or ever. Neither did my sisters. They were all serious girls, and they married well, to fine men. One sister was killed in Bosnia during the partisan war [a civil war in which Tito's partisan forces fought guerilla nationalist forces during World War II] as they were fleeing.

How did you meet your husband?

My father-in-law came to my father's house to ask for my hand in marriage for his son. I did not want to marry him, but they said, "By God, you will." And that was it. That was during the Austrian war. I never saw him before. He was in his 20s, but I did not want to marry because you never knew if he would be killed. I did not like the idea of being a widow. But it was my fate to be one—twice.

Talk about your wedding and your married life.

My *djever* and *barjaktar* came to my house. My brother brought me out of my house, handed me over to them, and they took me to my husband's village. We went on foot because there was a war and all the horses were taken by the army. His village was not too close to mine. I took a few little gifts with me. We did not have too much. Besides, because we are all poor, nobody expected too much of a gift. Just something little, out of respect. The wedding lasted two or three days. They roasted pigs and lamb. There was plenty of beer, but no dancing because we were in a war. Also, the men kept firing their guns, which is a tradition among *Crnogorci*.

Are you going to have a similar wedding for your son in America? It is different now. Today they [men] first try out the girl for a year or two, and if they do not like her, they send her back to where she came from. No, that is no good. It is much better to arrange a marriage. At least you know who you are marrying. Or, at least, your parents know before you do. My God, nothing is sweeter or dearer than pure love. When you have someone you love, you are never alone. But people in the big cities can tell you more about this than I can. In my day, very few people knew about love. We marry strangers, all of us—male and female. Males have a little better chance. He can refuse to accept his family's choice of girl. A girl cannot do that. Whatever she is told to do, she does. You probably cannot understand this. But it is the way it was.

I did not sleep with my husband for two months. Maybe it was even longer than two months. Sometimes I slept with my father-in-law, and sometimes with my sister-in-law. We slept in one bed. I did not have a mother-in-law. My husband had a brother who married earlier, but he did not live with us. My husband would tease me about him, "Heaven help you if that bear comes here. He would tear you apart." I never knew what he meant by that. But I am happy his brother was not around. Or maybe my husband was trying to scare me.

Was I afraid his brother would touch me? You do not know our customs. He would lose his life if he did. I told you before, this is an honorable land. Men were honorable then. Our people have good character. You could sleep with them for a year, and they would not touch you. That is the way it was then. No woman has to be afraid that someone will insult her. Women are protected here. I do not know how it is in America, but that is the way it is here. Things may be different today, still men protect the women in their families, and other men respect that.

Before you sleep with your husband, everyone in the house kisses you, male and female. You are dear to them until they see you with your husband, then they treat you differently. They are not as friendly. While you are still a virgin they are more playful with you. Once you go with your husband, they treat you more seriously. You are now truly married, and things are different. You are a married woman, even if you were married months ago. Now you are no more an innocent virgin.

Once, they once saw me with my husband, and they thought we were doing something [having sex]. Oh, I was so afraid, because I was not supposed to have contact with him until they told me I could. We even avoided looking at each other. There was always someone watching how you act. So you could not take a chance. Neither could he. First of all, he did not want to embarrass you in front of his family. I told you, our men show a lot of respect. After a couple of months, his sister told me to go to him when the time came. I do not know how they decided that.

He was such a good man. I can never forget him. Eighty years have passed since he was killed, and not a day passes that I do not think of him. I loved him because he behaved in an honorable way toward me. He never said a cross word to me. He never used an obscene word, nor did he ever insult me. Some men are dangerous. He was not one of them. We were only married for five years before he was killed. I cannot ever forget how kind he was. Such a good man!

After my first husband died, my daughter and I went back to my parents. My brother had been killed, leaving behind three orphaned children. I raised them. My parents were very old, so I had to take care of them.

When I was 30, I married a man who was not more than 27 years old. We had a simple wedding. He lived right here in the village, where he had a house. It was just a few houses away from mine. His family asked for my hand in marriage, but I refused him because I did not feel like getting married. Anyway, I liked him a little, so I married him. He was young, and he listened to me. If he was much older, maybe things would have been different. The first one [husband] is difficult, but the next one is like a body without a head. He, too, never laid a hand on me. Once he went to kill a pig and got his clothes all bloodied and dirty. I shouted at him, and he said, "I bet if you could, you would hit me." My job was to take care of the house and the animals. I also had the sewing machine, so I sewed a lot. He did other things. After he died, I never remarried. Two times is enough.

Did you have many children?

I had one daughter with my first husband and three sons and a daughter with my second husband. Few of them were born in the house, in bed. They were born away from the house in some shed, and when there was no one in the house, then in the house. We did not have children in hospitals. Having children is difficult. I did not give birth standing up, like some women. I leaned against something. I did see some women giving birth lying down. That cannot be easy either. There was usually no one around to help me. Afterward [after the birth], some neighbor would help.

My husband was of no help. When he saw me giving birth he would run away, because he was so frightened. He would call the neighbor. By the time he returned I would have wrapped up the baby already, and be sitting up like nothing happened. Most men are useless with anything to do with the home and children. I never heard of a man helping his wife have a baby. I do not think anybody else has either. Men are good for wars. Our men are good fighters. Brave soldiers. Thank God for that!

I gave birth to three children in two years, and I said to my husband, "You cannot come near me anymore, so go wherever you want. I cannot keep giving birth constantly. If you want it [sex], find someone. I cannot go on this way." If he found another woman, so be it. As long as he comes home to work I would say nothing. And when he wants to go, just let him go. Some men went then [to another woman for sex], as they do today. Not one man is normal. I am telling you. Not one. He would rather have a strange woman than his own wife. When they wanted to find that kind of woman, they could, because they were around. But some women go crazy when they learn their husbands go with other women. They say, "If he can go with other women, then I can go with other men." And some did. Men always went to married women. It was safer. [In the event she got pregnant, she could always claim the child's father is her husband.]

Was there a problem if a wife were unfaithful or a single girl got pregnant?

There were illegitimate children. She [the unmarried girl] gets pregnant and leaves the baby in front of city hall. They look for the mother, then they hand it over to the government to raise [to place in a home]. I never heard of a mother killing her child in this part of the country. My son's first wife told me that in some poor countries they kill such children at birth. Sometimes, even when the wife runs away with another man and leaves her husband and children, the husband kills the children. No, that does not happen in Crna Gora, only in other countries.

When a Montenegrin finds out that his wife has been unfaithful, he leaves her, but many pretend they do not see what is going on. Some even kill their wives. Last summer, a man in this village killed his wife with an axe in the head, then he slit her throat, and disappeared. He came back a little while later and hanged himself near the church. All kinds of things go on. Even here.

Were many rapes committed during wars?

The *Švabe* took away both males and females, and we never saw them again. But I never heard that they raped the women. First of all, we never went out in public. Some women were afraid, but the *Švabe* never caught them. They were more interested in having you work for them than anything else. They always treated those who worked for them fairly. There was a girl here who gave herself to anyone, and a song was written and sung about her:

> A Girl. A girl gave birth to a girl
> In Banok, in Bjelopavliće.
> She called to everyone in Babinje
> To everyone she gave a shirt.

[To "give a shirt" is an expression used when a single woman has premarital sex or a married woman has extramarital sex. So important are children that people in Serbia and Bosnia have been known to indulge in vicarious paternity. Milenko Filipovic, an ethnologist, writes in Among the People that in some villages in Serbia and Croatia a childless married woman, with the permission of her husband and mother-in-law, can go to the local village priest, whom she asks to pray for her, and "after prayer was over she asked him to 'turn her shirt over'" (120). She would then be taken to the monastery, where prayers were said for her and where she remained alone with the monks, who impregnated her. The child is treated by everyone as though it were that of the husband. Priests are chosen for such tasks because they can be trusted to keep a secret (119). There is no record of such a practice in Montenegro.]

Women like this were destroyed. That one made a mistake and none after her. That is the worst thing a woman can do. Still, some were suspected of going with men, even married women. Most times, when a husband finds out he divorces her or pretends he does not know what is going on. He just closes his eyes.

Did you socialize much with other women?

Oh, yes. We never socialized with women who flirted or went with other men. We knew who they were because our husbands told us about them. The men would come home and make fun of them. I am sure what they said was true. No one would dare say anything about an honorable woman. That would be reason enough for *krv* [blood revenge], if it came to the ears of the husband, his brothers, or her brothers. These are a very respectable and decent people. You could always pick out those other women. No one bothered with them, except the men when they wanted to have a good time. [From my understanding, "those women"—of which there were few—were often married women who, if they became pregnant, could claim the child was their husband's; "those women" also might be infertile women or those past child-bearing age.]

Did it ever happen that people married outside of their faith?

Some of our men married Muslim women. The families were very upset. She had to convert to our religion before he married her. But if Turks ever found one of our men looking at their women, they would kill him. Muslim women always wear white and live in cages [behind walls]. They even cover their eyes, so no one sees them. Now they go out without a veil. We never socialized with them or had anything to do with them, only our men did. When the Turks went to Skadar to fight, their women beat their chests. No, we never did that.

Sometimes one of our men would steal a Muslim girl and take her as his wife. Even if her family looked for her, they could never find her. She never went out of the house. She never worked outside the way we did. She had to stay inside all the time. Maybe her life was easier than ours, because she did not have to work outside. But you never know what goes on inside the house. No one ever saw her, except her children. I heard that sometimes she would meet with her family, but I do not know for sure. I just heard this.

You must remember a number of wars.

I remember the Albanian wars [Balkan Wars], two world wars [World Wars I and II], and the civil war [the civil war was a period during World War II when Tito's partisan, or communist, forces fought against Mihailović's Četniks, or royalists]. I went to Skadar during the Albanian war, just as it was ending. My brother was there as a cannoneer. My uncle, mother, and I went. We crossed over the *Skadarsko Jezero* [Lake Scutari] on a raft. We took him meat, eggs, bread, and whatever we had in the house.

We found them [the soldiers] in some hollow near the water. They were all black. They had been there for months. When we gave them the food and other gifts, they acted as if we had given them gold ducats. Some were dead, some were wounded. Many of the dead were still on top of the ground. There was no one to bury them. When it was over, some came home. Others went to Russia, and we never heard from them again. This is not an easy life. It is not easy.

My first husband was killed right there, right there in the woods. The guerillas saw him, got scared, and killed him. My family grieved for him terribly—they could not ever forget him—but I did not, though I could not eat for 15 days. I was angry with him for going up into the mountains where the bandits would see him and kill him. When we found him, he had a smile on his face. You would think he was still alive. You will not believe it, but he did.

When the *Švabe* were here, we could never give our soldiers any food.

Our men were held in camps, and when we went to see them we could not even give them a glass of milk. They were allowed to eat only what the *Švabe* gave them. If one of our men was caught taking food from us, they would beat him. I saw that happen. We went to see our men who were captured up there, and one of the *Švabski oficiri* [Austrian officers] thought we had given one of them something. They grabbed him, threw him to the ground, and began to beat him mercilessly. They beat him, but they could not kill him. They could not break him. He was down, and they kept beating and kicking him. Then they let him go, and another officer shot him by the side of the road. You see how we lived?

Did you know the *Švabe* would kill 100 of our men for one of theirs? Sometimes there would be 500 men in one pile. Then they would set them on fire. First they would take the ones from the camps. Then they would gather others from the villages. A truck would come and take them away. If they could not gather enough men, they took women and children. Of course children. They would then burn down the houses. They even put our men in a boxcar and set it on fire. We were always afraid, but you know how man is. What will be, will be. That is it. There is nothing else to do. They were stronger, so they could do whatever they wanted with us. But they had to leave after a while. I do not know what all of these people wanted from us. You could see we have very little. We even had less when they were here. Now we are rich. No one is hungry or naked. We have everything, and we have peace. Peace!

Did you experience much hunger during the wars?

During the *rat sa Švabama* [war with the Austrians] there was a lot of hunger. Anyway, we were never really hungry. Wheat was very expensive, and people were so poor that some unfortunate mothers watched their children die of hunger. People gathered nettles, which they cooked in whatever milk they had, instead of eating bread and cornmeal, none of which was around. You could not buy bread or wheat. Women made some kind of soup with a little salt and some little flour to thicken it. The soup looked a little better than water.

People lived terrible lives then. I saw many people die of hunger. A few men died right here. They found them on the side of the mountain. There was no bread or cornmeal for three years. Not only did our men die on the battlefield in Skadar, but they died on the way home. Their bodies were found alongside the roads. I saw it myself. Many of them. They [passersby] would only cover their heads with a little soil, but their legs and everything else were visible. At some spots I saw 25 dead men. That is a lot of dead bodies. I especially saw them during World War II and the civil war, when they were killed by their own people. Killed by their own people! During every war I saw dead people. War is war. War means killing and horror for everyone.

During the war, when the *Švabe* were here, even children caught stealing something like cabbage were killed by them. Do you know what cabbage is? The child was hungry and had nothing to eat, so he would take the cabbage or kale from someone else's garden, and they would kill him. That is the way it was here. They would kill a child for a head of cabbage. A hungry child! Auuuuuuuuuu! Kill a child for a head of cabbage! It must be hard for you to believe what I am telling you. It is the truth, *Bogami* [By God].

Of course children died from hunger. Piles of them. Whenever and wherever there was no food, they died. Of course they died. Those who lived in the mountains or near the mountains had a little wheat and some nettles. Those people had it better than those who lived below. In the mountains they could even have some animals and milk. Many of those people lived a lot better than those down here. In those houses down there [in the valley] no one could live, because there was nothing to eat. Nothing! People buried their own children as soon as they died, before they began to smell. Imagine rushing to bury your child before he rots!

Our people had to do whatever they were ordered to do, like prisoners. Whatever they [the enemy] wanted to do, they did. You know how it is. For them this is a strange land, an alien religion. Montenegro was always struggling with some foreign power. That is why it is called Crna Gora [Black Mountain]. Why is it called black? Because everything was done here. Everything was black here. Look what I told you. Everything black.

During the civil war, sometimes a son would kill his parents. If he did not do it, they would kill him. It was terrible here. Sometimes brothers were on two different sides. Who knows, maybe one even killed the other. The Italians and Germans were here, and the *Četniks* and the partisans. They were all killing each other. Everyone was here at the same time. So you can see how it was. It was *crno* [black]—Crna Gora! Now you know why it is called that. What else could they call it?

Sure, bombs fell around here. There was a neighbor who was running across the road with his cow when the bombs were dropping. He made it across, but his cow blew up with the bomb. Oh, yes. Cows were important. There was not much to eat anyway. During wars everything happened.

One thing I have to tell you. I have to tell you that the Germans behaved as adult men. They were fine men. They were brave soldiers. They did what they had to do and did not bother the people unless they were attacked. They were brave men.

What would you wish if I could give you one wish?

Peace. Today we have peace. I do not have to be afraid that someone is going to rob me. During the war you never knew when someone would come into your house and take everything. Here I am, all alone, and I have nothing to be afraid of. No one could strangle you now, here.

Thank you for sharing your thoughts with me.

Hvala tebe. Živa bila, ti i tvoji svi [Thank you. Long life to you and yours].

GOSPAVA

All of the women I interviewed were extraordinarily cooperative. At our initial meeting, Gospava appeared somewhat reticent, and I immediately had reservations about the outcome of the interview. As I sat at the dining room table with the coordinator, the driver, and members of the family eating and drinking, she joined in the conversation when drawn into it, responding as briefly as possible. To this point, I had completed 20 interviews successfully, so I was fully prepared for at least one to fail. I need not have been concerned. Gospava was eloquent.

Gospava is 101 years old. She lives with a number of people in a relatively small house. Because of their small size, most houses have no bedrooms as such, that is, rooms utilized exclusively as bedrooms. Every room—the kitchen included in some instances—is furnished with one or two couches, which convert to beds at night. To this day I remain awed by the cleanliness and order in every home. Except for an occasional wardrobe, closet space is nonexistent, yet there is no visible clutter. Where their clothing and bedding is kept remains a mystery I have yet to unravel.

Today, Gospava wears, as I had expected, the national dress of Montenegro. The few wisps of hair not covered by the black scarf tied around her head are iron-gray in color. Her hands are folded in her lap, remaining so positioned even when she speaks. She epitomizes the grace and dignity characteristic of her society. During the social period, I catch her eye several times, and we exchange smiles. Hers is a special smile, a curious smile—one that makes me eager to hear her story. As it turns out, she is eager to tell it. Now, alone, my tape recorder ready, I tell her that we can begin the interview.

Without waiting for my first question, she commences with her story. I suspect that she has given this moment serious thought, which is entirely understandable. Excluding her wedding day and the births and marriages of her sons, this is conceivably the only other day in her century-old life that she can enjoy center stage. The same can be said of all the women in this study.

Zorka: Tell me about your life in your natal village.

Gospava: Until I was 15 years old I lived with my parents and a deaf and mute sister. She was well under five years old. She had typhus, which destroyed a nerve. No doctor could help her. She is still living. I also had two brothers and two other sisters. One brother was killed in Bosnia during the war with the *Švabe*. The other was killed in Metohija, Kosovo, during the Balkan Wars. One of my sisters died from cancer, and the other one burned with her two children, one five years old and the other just an infant. She lived in her brother-in-law's house. The guerillas came to his house for supper, and he refused to feed them because he was afraid of the *Švabe*. The guerillas came back the next day and burned down the house with my sister and her children in it. Terrible things happened in this country.

During the time of the *Švabe* no men were around, so my mother asked a neighbor to help us out with planting crops. He was not fit for the army. But she came back saying, "My God, he does not want to help." So it was up to us, the women, to do everything. We had two cows. The oxen were taken by our army for food during the Turkish war. They were hungry. They needed food. I guess you know we were always at war with the Turks.

We always managed to have enough to eat. We had sheep and cows. We worked very hard. I plowed, cut wood, and did every other man's job. Even after I was married I did the same thing. We even built roads by breaking up rocks with a hammer. Here women work as hard as men, even harder. We do men's work, but they would never do women's work. So you can see that we never stopped working. We worked to live. We worked for our families, our sons, our children. Work. Work. Work. That is all we know.

How did you meet your husband?

I was 25 years old when I got married. He was 35. I never saw him before he came to ask for my hand. He never saw me either. He came with his brother-in-law. I saw him several times after that. Then you could not get married during Christmas Lent. So I was engaged for six weeks.

Did you kiss after you became engaged?

Kiss him? I never kissed him! Oh God, that would have been a terrible disgrace. Kiss him? Oh God, no!

I am going to tell you something. My husband really tricked me into marrying him. He was wounded in the Turkish war [interchangeable with Albanian war and Balkan war] and had pains in his legs. He could hardly stand on them. He waited until his legs healed, then he got married. I knew he was wounded, but I did not know about the pains in his legs. He wore a long shirt, covering his knees, and nothing showed. He did not limp either. If I knew that he was in that condition, I would have never married him. But I guess it was my fate. Fate is stronger than anything. [Montenegrins are strong believers in fate. Whatever happened in their lives is attributable to it.] Anyway, once I found out about his condition, it was too late. I could not do anything about it. Even if I did know, maybe they would have married me to him anyway. It is not easy to refuse the man your family says you have to marry.

Talk a little about your wedding.

I had a very nice wedding. At my home, when they [the wedding party] came to get me, my family had a dinner for them and my relatives. Only those from his family who come to get the bride and take her to her new family stay for dinner. I wore the Montenegrin national dress with a beautiful *ćemer* [woman's belt, decorated in silver], which I still have. There was not a finer one around here. They do not wear them anymore. All the girls who got married wore my *ćemer*, some even had their pictures taken with it.

I took a little gift to his family, stockings for the women and shirts for the men—all handmade. There were no stores. You could not buy anything, so we made everything ourselves. Everything we ate and wore was homemade. Even if there was a store, we were too poor to buy anything. There were lots of roast pigs and lamb, and so many other good things for my wedding. A wedding is an important day. You have to treat your guests with the best you have.

We lived in a huge house—one large room—with my two sisters-in-law and my husband's parents. My brothers-in-law and their families lived separately.

I spent the first night of my married life in the same bed with two brothers-in-law. That was the custom. A bride never slept with her husband the first night. She has to get used to her new family. They are all strangers to her, even her husband. We undressed like you do when you go to bed. But I was with them like they were my brothers. I was not afraid at all, anymore than I would have been afraid to sleep with my own brothers. That is one fear we do not have. We have honor. Men respect women. They protect us, not hurt us. Oh, God, no! It never happened that a brother-in-law touched his brother's wife. It is the way I told you, like sleeping with your brothers.

The second day my family, parents, and brothers visited. So that night I slept with my mother. After they left, I slept with my husband. Sure, I was a little afraid. After all, he is a strange man. I would have to be afraid. You would be afraid of going to bed with a strange man, no? Every woman would. He was such a good man. He was smart, even if he had no schooling. He worked the land. He even built a wagon for horses, which he drove to town.

How many children did you have?

I had 10 children. Seven are living, three died. I had my first child, a daughter, two years after I was married. My husband never said an unkind word when she was born. It is true everyone wanted sons, but he accepted her as what God wanted. He loved her like the sun. The next child was also a girl. She lived only for a year. She got the grippe and died. Many children died from the grippe. Very few children died at birth. They live, and later they get some kind of sickness and they die. Many times people do not even know what their children die from. There were no doctors. Mothers were the doctors. Other women were doctors.

After that I had a son, who died when he was two years old. That night he was fine, he played. We all went to bed, and I heard him moaning. I placed my hand on him, and he was cold. I called to my husband, "Nikola, Nikola, our child is dead." He said, "Did he choke?" "I do not know," I said. We never knew why he died. That is the way it happened to him. My husband was so happy when our son was born. Men came to congratulate him, and he served them coffee, *rakija* [brandy], and wine. They did not fire their guns because I never liked them to shoot, not even at weddings. I never liked too much celebration. I could never be too happy, no one could in this country. How could you be happy when you are always working, always tired, always poor?

I never gave birth in a hospital. I had them all at home, in the house. If any males were around, I would go off in a corner of the room and have the baby. I never had a baby outside of the house, but one of my sisters-in-law did. She was up in the mountain when her time came, and she had it right there. They named him Goran [mountain]. My mother-in-law helped with my births. She was a good woman, but very sickly. The woman is overworked here. She never stops, from early morning to late at night. She is the first one up in the morning and the last one to go to bed. It does not matter if she is sick or tired, she has to work. She has no time to rest. No one even knows when we are sick. We never complain. What is the sense. Who is going to listen?

How did you treat yourselves when you were ill?

We only took one child to a doctor. We nursed them ourselves. When someone catches cold, we take a frying pan, fill it with rocks, and heat it over a fire. Then we put some of the hot water in a bowl, cover the child's head with a blanket, and the steam cures him. We had no medicine. Tea, that is all.

Were you ever hungry?

We had plenty to eat, lots of potatoes, wheat, beans, meat, and yogurt. And we had livestock. We were hungry only when the *Švabe* were here. We almost died of hunger. We went out with our knives, searching for grass that would not poison us. We cooked and drained it. If someone had an animal and could get a drop of milk, they would add that to the grass and eat it. Those who had no milk ate it without, just plain cooked grass. That lasted a long time.

Many people died from hunger during the war. My sister and I found a dead man on our way to the city. We did not even try to help him, my God, out of fear. We could not even speak we were so afraid. Death is a big part of our lives. If we know about anything, we know about death and poverty. That, we know. That, we know.

Did the enemy ever rape the women?

The *Švabe* never raped the women. The army never raped. Neither did the Turks. Women were very afraid, but it never happened in Crna Gora. There were girls who did go with the soldiers of their own free will. That was not good for the family. Not good. I really cannot say if any were raped, because I minded my own business. So many children to take care of and to feed. I did not know what was happening outside of my own house. Too much work. Too much.

What happened when a woman was unfaithful to her husband?

It happened sometimes that a single girl had a baby. Today they send them somewhere, then it was not so. Let her family take care of it. I never heard that the family killed her, but I did hear that she drowned the baby. What is life going to be like for that kind of child in this country? Or for that kind of woman? Not too good, I tell you. That is a stupid thing to do.

When a woman could not have children, the husband often chased her out of the house. Some men kept her because they felt sorry for her. There were even men who brought another woman into the house. He must have children, so he has to do something about it. She cannot give him any, so maybe another one will. He cannot let his name die. If he does not have children, that happens. That is why children, especially sons, are important here. Very important.

If a wife was unfaithful, her husband got rid of her or he pretended he did not know what she was doing. He did not want to be disgraced if he could help it. That did not happen here. If it did, it was a rare thing. I never heard of it here. But it must have happened somewhere else. Not here.

Were women physically abused by their husbands?

Some men used to beat their wives, but only if she did something wrong. A woman was not allowed to be heard. Some men would lower the lid of a trunk on her hair [women rarely cut their hair], then he would beat her. She had to take it without ever complaining. If she did complain she would make it worse for herself, so she took it.

In my day I never heard of a husband killing his wife, but I know it happens today. Things are different today. Much different. People do not respect each other as they used to.

If someone in my family tried to beat me, I would struggle away from him. My husband never hit me. Why should he hit me when I did everything honorably and properly? But there are some jealous men, and that is why they beat their wives. Why should she take that? But she cannot do much about it. Husbands do what they want to do. All men do. Do they do the same thing in your country? Men are men. The worst thing among people is jealousy. In such a home there cannot be good fortune or goodness. Jealous people do stupid things. God forbid!

Some women who were beaten ran away from home, but they came back. Sometimes she feels sorry for him, and sometimes her parents send her back. Parents do not like to have their married daughters come back home. There was a Pavle [Paul] who always beat his wife. He was very jealous. Every time he beat her she would run away and then come back. He beat her so badly that she became sick. He took her to every hospital, but she died in the end. It was too late for her. He felt so terrible that he never remarried. No, he did not go to jail. Who is going to send him to jail? She is his wife.

When a woman leaves her husband she has to do with the children what the courts decide. [Gospava lives near a large city.] Daughters sometimes go with the mother, and sons always stay with the father. He carries his father's name, not the mother's. That is the way it should be. Maybe it is different in America. Sure, she feels bad. She may never see him again. Do you know how hard that is? Not to see your children again? What is he going to do with daughters? Some men keep them both. Not too many women in Crna Gora leave their husbands. He has to be very bad for her to do that. Mothers think first of their children, then themselves. Most times they never think of themselves. Always others.

Something just came to me. I heard of a widow who married her brother-in-law. But she had to be a widow first. She has children with him, but that is not very comfortable. People do not like that here. It is not going to be easy on the children, either. People talk. He is her husband's brother. Just like her brother. Even if he is not her *rod,* he is still a relative. Her husband's brother! From her *dom.* How much closer can you get? Like a brother! That does not show much respect. Eh? Some people do everything, even if it disgraces the family. Some people do not think and do not care. Thank God, that kind of a situation is very rare. Very rare.

You have buried so many of your loved ones, you must grieve terribly.

In my time it was a disgrace for a woman to cry for her husband, even for a tear to be seen, even for a son. I did not shed a tear for my husband when he died. You know when I shed a tear for him? It was when I went to get my pension. It was very crowded in the office, and everybody was pushing me. And I thought to myself, "Oh, if my husband was alive they would not be pushing me." At that moment I cried. I had no one to protect me. I had no one left but a brother-in-law. Everyone else went their way. I told you that *Crnogorke* [Montenegrin women] are protected by their husbands. Of course she has to behave and give him respect. He is her husband. Her husband. You have to respect a husband.

Scratch my face for my husband when he died? Scratch myself? God forbid that I would scratch myself for my husband! I did not shed even one tear. Some women did a little for their husbands, but more for their sons. That is the worst pain in the world. A brother is even worse. There is no pain like losing a brother. I hope you never know that.

You talked about your difficult life. If you could have one wish now, what would it be?

I wish for my family to live without sickness, and I would like to die tomorrow so I suffer less. I have lived too many years. Too many years. It is no good to live this long. No good. No good.

Thank you very much.

Bog ti dao zdravlje [May God grant you good health].

PART 3

The Friend of My Enemy Is My Enemy

> Mama *is humanity's universal word. When a mother's voice leaves our midst, in its place lies silence. Mother is Truth; all else is suspect. Women in Sparta taught their sons that only the sun was mightier than a Peloponesian. Our mothers taught us that honor is greater than a Peloponesian and the sun:*
>
> *Land for a head!*
> *A head for Honor!*
> *Honor for nothing on earth!*
> —Son's eulogy at mother's grave, from Todor Baković's Deprisivni
> Optimizam Crnogoraca

Every woman in this study survived numerous wars about which she has vividly painful memories. Each war brought with it a new foreign enemy, a new oppressor supported by powerful forces, joining the Turks, who had oppressed Montenegrins for 500 years. Even the disintegration of the Ottoman Empire in the latter part of the nineteenth century failed to end the historical hatred between Turks and Montenegrins. Montenegrins refer to all Muslims in their country as Turks for ecclesiastical reasons. These "Turks" are native-born Slavs who converted to Islam for economic and political reasons. Essentially, what the Montenegrins had experienced since the conversion of the first Turks five centuries ago was oppression by their "own" people, Slavs who chose to adopt an alien faith. Montenegrins do, however, make distinctions between Albanian Muslims and "native" Muslims. Albanians are not Slavs; therefore, they are merely referred to as Muslims or Albanians. Only 10 percent of Albanians are Roman Catholic and 90 percent are Muslim.

Jovana, whose interview with me fills this entire part of the book, lives peacefully in an area with a sizeable population of Slavic Muslims. The groups respect one another, each visiting the other on the other's respective holy days and festive occasions. Such was not the case for many years. For much of Jovana's childhood and young adult life these local Slavic Muslims were the arch enemy. Centuries-old hatreds had not been resolved, and fighting continued as Montenegrins struggled to wrest themselves from the yoke of oppression. During the occupation by the Austrians, "Turks" remained loyal to the new power rather than join forces with their countrymen against a foreign ruler. The Austrians, who replaced the Ottomans after the signing of the Congress of Berlin in 1878, found in the "Turk" a compliant, made-to-order ally.

The atrocities perpetrated on Montenegrins by the native-born Slavic "Turks" at the turn of the century—and sanctioned by the Austrians—are painfully and plainly detailed by Jovana.

JOVANA

Jovana, at the age of 102, is a most engaging, free-spirited woman. She shared her life experiences while smoking a cigarette and having an occasional drink of *šlivovica* (plum brandy). Her recounting of minute details of extremely painful and brutal incidents is riveting. Most fascinating are the eloquence and fluidity with which she articulates her history to absolute strangers from a foreign land. To learn that she had been rehearsed for the interview would not be surprising, except that she had no prior knowledge as to what it would entail. I find this charming centenarian to be mesmerizing.

Jovana entered my life by means of a guest at the American Center in the capital during its tenth anniversary celebration. Notables from academe and politics, and those of prominence in the arts and sciences, were in attendance. The director of the American Center, David Park, and his wife, Dr. Anna Maria Park, made a concerted effort to introduce me to those in attendance, expanding the network of acquaintances who might lead me to the population I sought. To my good fortune, Jovana surfaced.

She lives in the Brda region, in a village that had been under Turkish and Austrian occupation for centuries. Many Muslims, or *poturice* (Christian converts to Islam), also live in the area and have friendly relations with their non-Muslim neighbors. Arriving at Jovana's home in midmorning, the driver, the coordinator, and I are met at the end of the unpaved road leading to her house by not fewer than 10 relatives. She is not among them. After exchanging greetings with the men and kissing the women three times, we enter the house. Consisting of several well-appointed rooms, the house is relatively new. It is adjacent to an old, low structure—the original house, the one to which Jovana came as a bride.

Meeting Jovana is analogous to meeting royalty—a queen. She arises when we enter, shaking our hands and kissing us in the traditional way. Tall and elegant in her traditional native dress, she joins us all in a glass of *šlivovica*, requesting a cigarette shortly thereafter. Her family happily indulges her, encouraging her to be herself by offering her a drink and a cigarette. It is obvious from the onset that she is enjoying the attention being lavished upon her, and I immediately intuit that this will be a most productive interview. I was right.

Jovana lives with her son, his wife, and several other family members. Everyone sits around a large dining-room table, except the younger women, of whom I recall three, who set before us a sumptuous spread of *pršuta* and other smoked delicacies, young and aged cheeses, sauerkraut salad, hard-boiled eggs, yogurt, and freshly made bread served warm—staples in every Montenegrin home. These women never join us, remaining in the kitchen, observing us and replenishing the food as necessary. They take an avid interest in the conversation, smiling but never participating.

The men inquire about my background, genuinely astounded by my command of their language. Though never verbalizing it in so many words, it is fairly obvious that they are not at all clear as to my interest in their oldest women, to whom, though respected, little attention is given—certainly not to this degree. The ultimate purpose of my research bewilders them. When I explain that I plan to enlighten the world as to their little-known culture and proud history, they beam with pride.

An hour later, refreshed and sated, Jovana and I are escorted by her son to a comfortable room where the interview takes place. She is as I had anticipated: animated, enthused, and anxious to answer my questions. Typical of her generation and her society at large, she responds promptly and confidently, never faltering or groping for a word. Language—logical, intelligent, focused—pours forth. Jovana is a shining star. Periodically, she takes time out during the course of conversation to have a drink of *šlivovica* and a cigarette, but not before offering the same to her guest, ever conscious of that notable hallmark of her culture, hospitality.

Zorka: Tell me when you were born and about your natal family.

Jovana: I really cannot tell you the date when I was born. I know I was born in May, but I do not know the date because I never went to school. Yes, I know the year. In May I will be 103 years old. I had a cousin who was born at the same time. He died, and on his tombstone is written how old he was. Since I was born in the same month and year as he was, I know I am 103 years old.

I had brothers and sisters, but I do not have any now. They are all dead. I am the only one still living. There were six of us, and then our mother died. I was almost nine years old when she died. All I know is she got sick and then died. She never went anywhere. I was the oldest of the daughters. Two of my sisters died when they were little. One died at birth; she was not even baptized. The other was a little older. Thank God they did not live.

Why thank God? Because they died when they were little. Why should they live and suffer in poverty? Do you think it is easy living in this land? You do not know what it is like in this land for a girl. Everyone is sad when she is born. Why? They know what her life will be like. Outside of the work they can do, nobody really cares much for them. I do not mean they beat her, but no one pays any attention to her. The men in the house treat her as if she is not there. Even brothers do not pay much attention to her. They [males] only notice her if they need her to do something for them. But she gets used to that. Maybe it is a good idea to be treated like that. Then you are prepared when you get married. You know what you have to do. You also know that everything you do will be for someone else. Even though my mother died when I was nine, I already knew what I had to do.

But you know what? Every man in the house would protect her with his life if anyone did anything to her or insulted her. That is true. Everyone will tell you the same thing.

Mothers cry when they give birth to a girl. Fathers are even more unhappy. Everybody wants sons. After a daughter is born the house is sad, like when somebody dies. It is like a funeral. Poor mothers blame themselves because they disappointed their husbands and the clan. You will not believe this, but it is true. Ask anyone. Fathers apologize when a girl is born. How does he apologize? *Sine,* I will tell you. They still do it. When someone asks him what was born in his house, he says, "Forgive me, I had a daughter," or "Forgive me, I had a child." See that? Do you understand? He is ashamed that he has a girl!

Eeeeeee, it is different when a son is born. He never calls him a child. He calls him "*sin*" [son]. He will proudly say, "*Rodio mi se sin*" [A son was born to me]. Everyone knows it by that time anyway, because the first thing he does is fire his gun. The whole village knows what happened in his house. The only thing they do when a girl is born is cry. At least the women do. This happened to me just as it did with every other girl.

Crna Gora is not an easy place for any of us. My brother also died when he was little. He was four years old. He died from his stomach. He got sick and died. That is all. Only three of us were left, two brothers and me. Even though I was little myself, I raised my brother. Oh God, how we suffered! Terrible suffering. That is why I said my dead sisters are lucky. I know you cannot understand this because you were born in America. In this land, if you live you suffer. The lucky ones die.

My mother gave birth to her children wherever she could. There were no hospitals then. The children were all born outside of the house. Where else? How else? You were not allowed to have children in the house. Everybody knows that. You could not dirty up the house, so she had to have her baby outside, even in the snow. Then she brings it in, takes it to a priest to get holy water. She washes the baby in that water for 40 days. That was the custom.

My poor mother! Her marriage was arranged like everyone else's. She did not know her husband either. She was no different from all the other women. She did not like the person she married either. But who asked her?

My father stayed a widower for three years. My uncle and his wife took care of us. My uncle was very good. My father married a woman who had no children. She raised us and took care of us. It would be a sin to call her *maćeha* [stepmother]. She was so good.

We played as children, but we worked more than played. I began working the moment I could pick something up with my hands. Peasants and my relatives paid me to work. I cleaned fields and spread manure for a little money. My father never hit me. Never! Well, he did once, but I deserved it. I cannot remember what I did. I just know it was my fault. I guess I remember it because fathers did not usually hit their children. Mothers did that. That is because she is tired and overworked.

My mother, like all women, was the first one up in the morning and the last one to go to bed. She could never be sick. She is in charge of the house. When she got sick, she died. No one ever heard her complain. We are not like that. And what good would it do if you did? You work until you cannot work anymore, and then you die. Work, then die. That is what life is like in Crna Gora. The father is almost like a guest in his own home. He was a brave man; both my uncle and father were good men. During the war my father received the Miloš Obilić medal [medal for bravery]. That was when Crna Gora was at war with the Turks.

Talk to me about your marriage.

I do not even know how old I was when I got married. I must have been around 18 years old. My husband's family made an agreement with my father and uncle, and they gave me to him. Refuse? Refuse to marry him? I could never say no to my father. In those days whatever your father told you to do, you did. You could never say you did not want to marry the man they picked for you. They made the arrangements, and you went along without complaining. So I got married. Just like that.

My husband gathered his family and relatives for the wedding. We were together for six weeks. On a Sunday, six weeks from the day I entered their house, the *Švabe* captured him and took him away. He was imprisoned for three years. Those who lived were released from prison, and he was one of them. He started on his way home through Serbia and was never heard from again. No one knows what happened to him, or where his bones are. Our lives are nothing but suffering. I told you that.

I was not pregnant. I had to wait seven years before I could get married again. That was because I did not have my husband's death certificate. Of course it was the custom for a bride to spend the first night of her marriage with her brother-in-law or some other member of the family, anyone except her husband. Some women sleep with their mother-in-law, father-in-law, or a sister-in-law. Most times it is with a brother-in-law. But I did not have to do that. They would not let me sleep with my brother-in-law. Yes, I had one, but they kept me away from him. Yes, it is strange, and I never found out why. No one ever told me, and I would not dare ask. So they let me spend the first night with my husband in a small room of our own.

My mother never told me what to expect when I first slept with my husband. I did not know what was going to happen. No, I did not tell my daughter either. In those days people did not talk about such things as they do today. That is a big change. Today they meet on the road and get married. If I had ever gone somewhere away from my home, I could never return. That is the way my parents were.

I really was not afraid of my husband, because I already knew him. He was my neighbor. As a matter of fact, he used to say to me before we were married, "I would rather grab a snake by the tail than touch you." That is the kind of person I was. No one could say a word to me. I mean, no man could say a word to me. Did I love him? Well, I can tell you there were many men who wanted to marry me. But he was a good man.

Yes, I know that some men covered the faces of their brides when they wanted to sleep [have sex] with them, but my husband did not do that. [When a man wants to have sex with his wife, he may cover her head with a heavy, lace-like scarf, hanging near the bed, and she silently submits.] What? A husband rape his wife? [So alien was the concept of "rape" in a marriage that she took some time to mull it over, but still could not grasp its meaning.] Refuse him? You could never say, "No, I do not want to!" He is stronger, and he is your husband. Sure he [the second husband] would hit me. You do not ever refuse your husband. You just do as he tells you. There is no other way for us here. He hit me with a broom we kept in a corner of the room. Sometimes the day would pass, and I would say, "Spasoje, we did not do anything today." Then he took the broom and beat me. Just for saying that! But it did not happen too often. He never hit the children. He never wanted to, even if they needed it.

After my first husband was taken away and did not return, I stayed on living with my brother-in-law and my father-in-law, who was 100 years old. They both died within two days of each other. Imagine that! My jetrva [brother-in-law's wife] stayed here with me for two years after her husband's death, until she could not take it anymore. This was not a happy home. Too much tragedy and death. I did not return to my parents, but stayed on in my dom.

Once the seven years were up after my first husband's disappearance, another marriage was arranged for me by one of the most famous men in Crna Gora. He was, how would you say, a legend. He gave me away without even asking my father or me. My father, a mailman, went to the pijac [marketplace] and he [the legendary man] said to him, "We gave away your daughter." "To whom?" he asked. They told him, and he just scratched his head. "Do not scratch your head. We gave her away," they told him. He merely answered, "Well, since you already gave her away, I also give her. *Uzela je mutna voda."* ["Let the muddy water take her," or "To hell with her," used as a display of manliness, a show of strength before this hero, respect for a "legend." In reality, however, his heart may have been breaking. In this tribal warrior patriarchy any public demonstration of affection, especially toward a female, is a sign of weakness unbecoming a warrior.]

My second marriage was good. He was 50 years old when I married him. I was around 25 or 30. He was a widower, with a child from his first marriage. Many women died in childbirth. This is not a good place for women. The lucky ones leave only one child behind, but, sadly, some leave many children for someone else to take care of. It would have been very hard for me to get married if I had children. It is much easier for a man, even if his life is not that easy either. But he keeps his children. A widowed mother has to leave her children behind if she remarries. They belong to their father's family. Anyway, no man wants to raise another man's children. He will take the woman home so she can take care of his children. But she cannot take hers with her. Do you know how hard that is? Leaving your children behind, maybe never to see them again? Always thinking of them, but never able to say a word. That is the custom here. Men do not want what other men made. I found a three-month-old child here, and I raised him with a coffee spoon [a metaphor for careful nurturing]. There he is today, with his own children.

How many children did you have, and where did you have them?

I had five children with my second husband, two girls and three sons. My first child was a son. Having only daughters is terrible here. One of my relatives had 10 daughters and no sons. That was not easy. She raised them all and married them, except one stayed with her, and one she lost when it was a child. The birth of a daughter does not bring much joy. The first and second can be tolerated, but having a third is very bad. Females are not too welcome. We *Crnogorci* delight in males. Yes, even women. Sons are wealth and joy in a house. Even having 10 sons is not too many.

Oh God, my first son was happiness and good fortune! How would he not be? I gave birth to him in the kitchen. [It was customary to have a summer kitchen, essentially a small shed near the house. Summers can be relatively hot and oppressive.] I knelt down on my knees, and with the help of my *jetrva,* who knew what to do, the baby came out, and everything was fine. I had another son in the kitchen also, the same way as my first. I had prepared thread and a knife beforehand, then I cut the cord and tied it. I had sons, two daughters, and a stepson. I love this boy as much as my own. If I was ever able to get any candy, I would divide it among the children, but not before I gave him some—he before my own children, always.

I gave birth to one daughter right over there in that field which you came over. It was winter and the snow was deep, almost up to my knees. I had her, took her home, and nothing happened to her. I had tied some firewood to my back, and my pains came. I could not take the wood off my back because I would only have to tie it back again. So I went up to a tree, put my arms around it, stooped a little, and the baby came out. Then I raised myself a little, so the baby would drop and pull out the afterbirth. I wrapped her up in my apron and brought her into the house. My oldest daughter was there, along with my second child and my husband's child, the one I raised. They took down a straw mattress for me to lie down on. They found a knife so I could cut the umbilical cord, which I did before I lay down. [Obviously, she walked home with wood tied to her back, carrying a newborn baby still attached to her.] Believe it. That is the way it happened. My *jetrva* learned from a doctor that when a child comes out with the umbilical cord, it also pulls out the afterbirth, and everything is clean. I remembered what she said, and that is what I did.

My husband, who had been working in front of the house, came in and said, "Why are you lying down, Jovana?" I told him why, and I knew he was not going to be happy because the baby was a girl. And he was not. He just walked away when I told him I had a girl. So I got up immediately, went over to do some wash, and bring in some water.

Did your husband help you?

He, help me? I felt ashamed that I was lying down, even if I was so tired. I know I brought home firewood and a baby, but that does not matter. A woman is expected to do all that, and everything else. And do you know what? Nothing happened to her or to me. We are both still alive.

My other daughter was born in the barn. I was so tired from the day before. I had done the work of three or four people, when a cousin came to visit and sat around for hours. He asked me to make him some coffee, but I did not have the strength to do it, so he left. The next day my husband, knowing how much I had worked and how tired I was, said, "This morning, do not work down there on the plums. It is raining. I will go." And he left, but I could not sleep. My cousin came back, asking for a crowbar he needed to drive in a post. I thought about where I could get a crowbar. And I am beginning to get labor pains. He is calling, and I am in pain. Terrible pain. I go to the barn to look for a crowbar, and the pains are getting worse. I leaned against a saddle to get some relief from the pain.

No sooner than he went into the house, my girl was born. What am I now going to do? I pulled it out, and it drops easily. Pains? Who asks you? I bathe it, wrap it up, and let it sleep. I first put her in a pail of cold water.

Muslim Albanian Anifa Zagora, 102 years old, in her garden. *Zorka Milich*.

Tole Dedvuraj, a 104-year-old Roman Catholic Albanian (Malësian), in her living room. *Zorka Milich*.

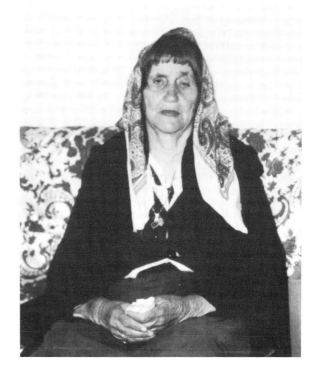

Milica Božović, 115 years old, is one of the two oldest women in Montenegro. Every summer, along with her extended family and livestock, she climbs up into the mountains, where the animals graze and the family camps until fall. *Zorka Milich.*

102-year-old Andja Milatović pitching hay with a wooden pitchfork. An avid gardener, she grows her own fruits and vegetables, which she harvests and stores for winter provisions. *Mark W. Milich.*

Milosava Coguric, 103 years old, stoically concealing the pain of a broken hip. She lives in a breathtakingly picturesque area, beneath snowcapped mountains overlooking a cavernous ravine, but she and the other villagers frequently experience loss of livestock and produce to wild boar and eagles. *Mark W. Milich.*

Stanija Radenović at 104 wearing the traditional dress of Montenegro in which she was married and in which she will be buried. *Mark W. Milich.*

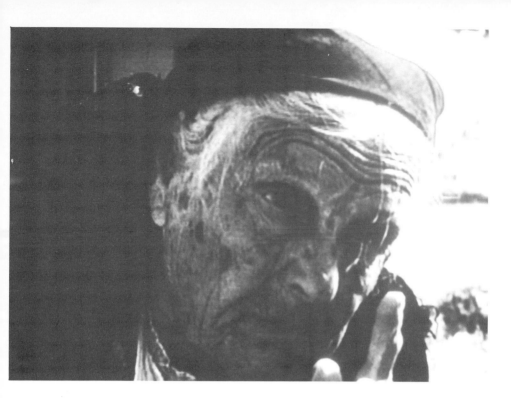

Jove Bracanović, 103 years old, in her garden. *Mark W. Milich.*

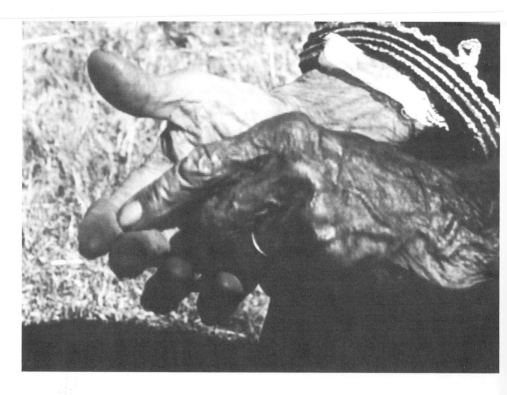

The hands of Jove Bracanović. *Mark W. Milich.*

She started to move around, and she is still that way. Yes, cold water, that is all I had. I bathed her, and then I lay down. Spasoje came home and said, "Why are you lying down? And I said, "Because I feel like it." He looked at me, "What do you mean, you feel like it?" "Yes, my God. Here she is," I said. And I stayed where I was. Oh, how I suffered giving birth to these children. No, he was not angry when I gave birth to a girl. Maybe he was, but he never showed it. He loved the oldest daughter more than he loved his sons.

I breast-fed my children to the very end, and I did not do it not to get pregnant. I just felt sorry for the little ones. The son that was killed used to call me, when he was two or three years old, as I left to visit my family, "Jovana, give me your breast and then go." [It is not unusual for male children to call their mothers by their first names. It is something of an adult, manly gesture.]

How did you lose your children? Your husband?

I lost my oldest son when he was 18 years old, during what I call the Albanian and Austrian war [Balkan Wars and World War I], which ruined this area. We were refugees here, and they beat him with the handles of their guns. They broke his lungs. He suffered for 15 days, and we had nothing and could do nothing. I went among the people, begging something for him. As he lay dying, he spoke to me. He started to move his lips. I called to him by his nickname, "Datko, do not be angry with me. But I do not hear you very well. You said something to me, but I could not hear it." He answered, "I did not say anything, Jovana." Again I said, "Did you call me, son?" He called alright, but his *duša* was gone. Tears formed in my eyes, but I did not want to cry in front of him, and then he quietly gave up his *duša*. He suffered so much. They did not kill him with lead [a bullet], so he had to suffer long. Everything happened here.

I never shed a tear. But I cried wherever I went, but not so anyone could see me. At his funeral I sat next to his coffin, and I said to myself, "Let him go. I will not cry, even if he is my first." But I did cry, wherever I went. He did not want to come for me [take her with him in death]. "You will know," he said before he died, "if I recover, how a mother should be taken care of." He never had a chance to show me. That was our fate.

My husband died when he was 63 years old. He died in my arms. There were other people in the house at the time. I held him until my arms ached, and I said to someone, "Ljubo, take him." He took him just as his *duša* left him. He had an ulcer, which burst. [Many deaths were attributed to ulcers, which may have been cancers. A common comment on the cause of death is that the person died from a "sore that would not heal" or a "stomach ulcer that burst."] Oh, my God, yes! Many people here have ulcers. Something latches on and makes an ulcer. He had a huge funeral. No one had more people. And the people said, "How are these children going to grow up?" It would have been easier if they had been about 10 years old. The oldest was about 10, and the youngest was in the cradle. All so young and poor!

Oh, there was a lot of wailing at his funeral. That is our custom. All the people in the village and all the refugees were there. Men and women go to a funeral and wail. Here, we do not have *tužbalice*. Why should I scratch myself and beat myself? Some women do it because they are stupid. Why else? He [the husband] was here and left, so let him go. They carried his body on their shoulders to the grave, which was far away. We wear black practically all our lives because we are always in mourning for some relative.

The death of a son or a brother is the worst pain in the world. Oh, my God! My God! To a sister no one can be dearer in this world than a brother. Maybe a grandson could be equally as dear. A grandson is dear to everyone. Still, no one can be nearer or dearer than a brother. A brother is a brother! My brothers died on me. Oh, oh, oh, my God! To be without a brother! To lose a brother! Not to have a brother anymore! When he is no longer there! When you lose a brother you cannot get another one. Neither can a son be replaced. Well [laughing], a husband is different. You could always get another one if you want to. But a son or brother? Never!

What kind of a social life did you have?

We socialized on special days like our *slava*. My maiden *slava* was *Nikolj Dan* [Saint Nikolas' Day], and here [husband's *slava*] it is *Elijn Dan* [Saint Eli's Day]. It was a big celebration, like a wedding. We prepared a lot of food and had a good time. I especially had a good time when I went to my relatives [natal village] for their *slava*. There were many guests in the room, and I was very well liked by the whole clan. I would take a glass of *rakija* [brandy] and sing.

I still have a glass of *rakija* every morning, before I have coffee. Like then, we always have guests in the house. No, it was not shameful for a woman to drink. They drank a glass or two. That is not drinking. I started to smoke much later. I have been smoking for 30–35 years. Now, I cannot be without it. It is as if somebody is forcing me to do it. Miško [a grandson] tells me to cut down on my smoking, but I cannot.

Can we stop now, so I can have a cigarette and, maybe, a little drink? . . . Ever since I started to smoke, I smoke these factory-made cigarettes. Before, I used to roll them, but I never smoked them. Oh, yes, I smoke a lot. My grandson keeps telling me that I am going to poison myself. Poison myself! There is nothing wrong with me. He keeps saying, "But, *Baba,* you will poison yourself." Look, I am still here. He buys cigarettes for me. Who else would buy them? Just Miško and my great-grandchildren. I also get a lot of tobacco as gifts. I have a pile of it right over there [pointing to table in corner]. I do not do anything, so I get bored and smoke. I sometimes watch TV, but when we go to the *katun* there is no TV. I just go home to sleep. During the day we stay at the *katun,* where we make *šlivovica* and do other work. I come back here to sleep, but my grandson and some of the others stay up there.

Oh, I am so lucky. No, I cannot have that one; it is too strong. I do not like strong *rakija.* No, no, you cannot get through there, I will get it. [She insists on getting the brandy she wants.] I know which one I like. Just stay seated. Ooooooooo, this is good! This is good *rakija!* Good *rakija!* No, no, I will pour it myself. There is plenty of *rakija.* Take some for yourself. It is good. [Toasts.] *Zdravo bila* [May you be healthy]! *U zdravlje* [In good health]!

You were still a young woman when your second husband died. Did you remarry?

Yes, when my second husband died I was still young, and many men wanted to marry me. But how could I leave five or six children behind just to get married. I am not crazy. Who would take care of my children if I got married? They had no grandfather or uncle. No one. I would rather hang myself than leave them behind. Some women committed suicide when they left their children behind. They do it by drowning. Something happens to her, and she kills herself. I could understand that. I personally do not know of any cases, but I heard it happened. Leave my children? How could I leave my children to cry and to go hungry, just to be married? Even if having a man was important to me, it is more important to have a house full of children than one man.

What happens when a woman is infertile?

When a woman cannot have children, sometimes her husband feels sorry for her and keeps her. And sometimes a good wife tells her husband to take another wife. The first wife goes back to her parents. They arrange a marriage for her with a widower who already has children. She raises his children and is not a burden to her own family.

Even when a woman only has daughters it is hard for her. She suffers very much. It is hard for Montenegrins when there is no male child. Some men keep these women, some get rid of them. Such women resign themselves to their fate. Their lives are not easy. You can imagine what it must be like for her. Everybody knows she cannot have sons. In a land where sons are prized and daughters are not, her life is hell.

When he brings in another wife—that is, when the first is childless—the two wives stay in the house. The first one to have a son stays with him. The other has to leave. That is a terrible situation. God forbid! You would not wish that on the worst person. What a life!

Were there any incidents of infidelity or premarital pregnancy in your day?

When a single girl gets pregnant, she gives birth to a bastard. She has to keep the child, but nobody wants her. She cannot do a thing about it. Sure, some of these babies were killed. I know of such cases. She has a baby and drowns it. Dead babies were found, and nobody knew who they belonged to. She sure is not going to say anything. All she can do is hope that nobody finds out that it is hers. Then she would have to kill herself, or maybe her brother would [kill her].

An unfaithful wife disgraces everyone, just like the single girl who gets pregnant. The wife is thrown out of the house. Her parents do not want her either. But sometimes they take her back, and she becomes a *rob* [slave], without respect. No one pays any attention to her. They ignore her as if she is not alive. And that is how her life passes. Sometimes they kill themselves, or some member of the family kills them. Honor and reputation is everything in this country. So you have to protect it.

Do you recall any interfaith marriages?

Some Montenegrin men did marry Muslim girls. It is too bad! But our women married Muslims more than Muslim women married our men. That is not good, because the other faith is evil. The Turks were evil. When they saw a good Serb, they did everything in their power to kill him. In the next village there was not one young man who died a natural death. They all died by a gun, a Turkish gun. That is the way people lived then. Among the Turks, a widow could marry her husband's brother. Did you ever hear of such a thing? Disgusting! Some men married their sisters-in-law or their aunts. Imagine! Aunts! They are much different people.

I must tell you though, our men never married a Muslim girl unless she converted. Once she took our faith, she was accepted. Look, sometimes a man sees a beautiful woman and he wants her, even if she is of another faith, like Muslim. That did not happen too often. Families were very unhappy when a son did that. I think you would be too, no? Everybody would. Your own is your own.

One of our men in the village married a Muslim woman, and she converted.

There was not a better woman in this area than she was, believe me. She appealed to him because she was a good woman, an honorable woman. They [the male members of his family] went to get her. She jumped out of the house and ran off with them. They took her away to their house. How could her family look for her when they did not know where she was?

I never heard of Turks raping girls then, nor did they ever kill a woman with a gun. There was honor even among them. Now everything happens.

Did Montenegrin men marry gypsies?

One of our men marry a gypsy? God forbid! I never heard of it, and I do not think I ever will. A gypsy? God, no!

Were there any Jews around here?

Oh, yes, there were Jews here. But they did not hide their faces [referring to the veils worn by Muslim women]. They did hide their women from the Serbian people. Who knows why? Probably because they had another religion. Only the devil would know why. They never bothered anyone. They stayed by themselves.

Did the Turks around here have harems?

I do not know if they had harems. Of course, *jadna* [poor thing], they had three, four, or six wives. A Selović had six wives, six wives for one man! The Selovićes were a Turkish tribe. The women dressed as *bule* [veiled women] and wore *dimije* [pantaloons]. They were always dressed in white. Now they do not do any of that. [Tito forbade the wearing of veils by Muslim women.] They do not cover their faces, nor do they wear *dimije*. But some still wear white scarves on their heads and *dimije*. [Montenegrin women cover their heads with black scarves, differentiating them from Muslim women, who wear white scarves, exclusively.] Let me tell you, some of them were beautiful. Like everywhere else. But how could you tell when they were always covered up? I am just guessing.

When one of them, from a distance, saw me walking down the road, she quickly covered her face. Even if I am a woman, it did not matter. She covered it from a woman, too, let alone a man. They called that *valet*—it was some kind of sin to be seen by anyone except members of the immediate family. Who the devil knows why? Strange customs!

So, this Selović had six wives, and he slept with every one of them. He slept with one for a week, and then he would go to the next one, until he had slept with all six. Then he would start all over again. The one he was with prepared his clothes, and he walked around the village all dressed up. Just like that. I do not know how many rooms he had in the house. My God, how would I know? Who knows how many children he had! There must have been too many. Those people have a lot of children. But so do we.

Oh, yes, Muslim women used cosmetics. Of course they did. When you passed them they smelled. They stank so much you could not go near them. Who knows why they smelled? It was something they put on their faces. It was something they thought would make them prettier for their husbands, and everyone else. [She meant that the Muslim woman who used cosmetics did so that she would be the prettiest in the household.] They tried to please their men. They did not work the way we did. They stayed inside most of the time.

Tell me about the relationship between the Slavic "Turks" and the Serbs.

I have to tell you something about the Turks. Whenever they wanted to kill a Serb, they did it—just like that. They especially liked to kill Serbs who were worthy. They killed them for no reason, just so he is no longer alive. That is all.

Of course they cut off heads. Our men cut off noses. They cut off noses with a sword. But the Turks, oh, no, they cut off heads. Our men took the noses to whoever was the leader at that time, so he could see them. Certainly I saw a man without a head. I did, I did, when I was a girl. I saw a neighbor without a head. First, the Turk killed him, then cut off his head. He took the head to Plav to show he had killed a Serb. The man's sister went to the Turk and asked for the head, and he gave it to her. First, the Turk asked her, "What is this head to you?" She said, "He is my brother. Do you need it anymore?" He answered, "No, believe me. Here, take it!" She took that head, wrapped it up in a scarf, took it home and shoved it into her brother's coffin. She loved that brother as only a sister can love a brother. My God! Sister for brother!

I am glad you came back today, because on the day you were here I did not think to tell about my *rodno selo* [natal village].

[I had interviewed Jovana privately several weeks prior to this particular day. I returned for a second interview with my son, who videotaped it. I have incorporated both interviews in this edited version.]

That was the most important thing I had to tell you, so you could write it down. It never came to my mind that day. But it is good for you to know, so you can tell other people about the massacre in Veliko—the terrible massacre, which happened when I was a young woman.

In two hours 750 victims fell in the town of Veliko. So many children were killed there. Who did it? Who else but the Turks and *Švabe*. They would hang a living child, around two or three years old, on a plum tree. They would hang him and skin him alive. The child would be screaming piercing screams as they continued to skin him. Do you hear what I am telling you? You hear? They did that to a child of one of my cousins. After that, they did the same thing to a neighbor's child. One of the neighbor's children was killed, and the other was skinned alive. After that they killed the whole family. Oh, yes, for two hours they killed 750 people. That has been written. And the day you were here we spoke about everything but that. Imagine!

They burned down houses and threw people on the fires in Veliko. Sixteen people in one house were locked up and burned alive. Human beings! Living human beings! In Oranica, a village below Veliko, there was a pregnant woman with two children, one sat by her side, the other was in her lap. They shot the woman and the child beside her. When they shot her, her son fell out of her lap. Then they lit the *ognište* [the hearth, a five-foot-square opening in the floor, approximately eight inches deep, used for heating and cooking] and threw her, her dead son, and the living one—two sons—into the fire and burned them all. People came to look at the blackened wall where children were burned. They burned people! Burned people! Everything happened in Veliko. To think that the day you were here that did not come to my mind. It is not easy being stupid! That is what happens to someone who is stupid.

I was visiting in Martinović at the time, another village, where my husband and brother-in-law escaped to save themselves from the Muslims. When I returned to Veliko, it was all over. My two *zaove* [husband's sisters] were also killed. They killed them against the wall of their house. Just like that!

In a house where a family of nine lived, all were killed. One of the women's mothers was visiting her daughter, and when she heard the machine guns mowing down the people, she fell, but was not shot. She fell under the dead bodies. Nine were killed in one family, but she was not among them. Two brothers of this family, who hid in the forest, came home at night to bury the dead. All night long they carried corpses, pushing them into the grave. Those two brothers did that all by themselves. How must they have felt? They married afterward. Their wives were among those killed in the house, so they remarried. They died many years later.

They killed whatever they saw, those *Švabe* and Turks. Oh, those devils! They killed women and children, pregnant women, too. They did everything. Skinned, butchered, and who knows what else. They burned them in their houses, so who knows what was done to them before that? God forbid! They did that to *žive duše* [living souls]! How could anyone do that to children and pregnant women? An uncle of ours, his wife, daughter, and two grand-children—all burned to death. Thrown into the *ognište!*

The Turks and *Švabe* took from us whatever they could—whatever little they found. But there was nothing to plunder. We had nothing. We are very poor people. Anyone could tell you that.

Now there is peace, *jadna*. It is peaceful, but some people are beginning to rise up. I do not know who they are. There are those who are rising in Plav. The police had to come from Titograd and other places to take care of the problem. [I interviewed Jovana in the spring of 1990.] This land is never in complete peace. Why is that? I do not know. But there is always somebody who is not happy and wants to change things. That is not always good. That is how fighting starts, and poor people suffer. We have suffered enough already. Everybody is tired. But I guess some are not.

I know that many young Montenegrin men went to America at the turn of this century. Tell me about that period.

Our men went to America because we were so poor. Only women stayed behind. It is said that they left to make some money, leaving behind old girls [unmarried women]. There was so much poverty here. Poor people all over the country. Some men came back, some never did. Some even left behind a wife and children and never returned. She had to raise the children by herself. Some men came back after they got old and sick. Their wives had to take care of them. All his life he spent away from his family, and when he is old he comes back. He did not even know his children. Never saw them. That happened also. Some women were pregnant when their husbands left, so that child never saw his father, does not even know what he looks like. Some earned a lot of money there. [She begins to sing:]

> America, they say, is a cursed country
> For taking away half the world
> For some little money,
> Leaving behind old girls.

[She explains the meaning of the song.] That man they are talking about who went away was a Montenegrin—a Montenegrin son. So many girls could never marry because so many men left for America. That was not good for them—not good at all. It is not good for people not to be married. Not good.

What was the happiest day of your life?

The happiest day of my life is today. I have grandchildren and great-grandchildren. I have sons. One came to visit me today, and he brought me a gift. I have 29 grandchildren [among whom were great-grandchildren and great-great-grandchildren], and the thirtieth will be here in March.

People live better today than we ever lived. I would not want to go back. I cannot do better than I am now. Nothing is missing. They take care of me. Only my bones ache. When I was taking a bath, I fell in the tub and hurt my hips and spine.

What was your worst day?

I really do not know how to tell you which were my worst days. They were all about the same. I already told you about life in this land. It is difficult. We were always poor. Mothers buried children because they had nothing to feed them, so they died of hunger. Mothers buried children who got sick, and there was no one to help them, so they died. Most times, no one knew what they died from. He dies, and you bury him. What else can you do? Life was never easy.

How do you account for your long life?

Who knows why I lived so long? A young man came here last fall to help with the reaping, and someone told him that I was over 100 years old. He was more than two meters tall; he stood up and came over to me and said, "How are you, *Baba*? What kind of food did you eat to live so long?" I told him that I ate the kind of food people in other countries never ate. He never said a word and went back to work. No people in any other country ate nettles and all kinds of grasses. There I was, a refugee for three years with half-starving children waiting to be fed, and there was no food. I would have jumped into the Lim [a river] if I was near enough. God forbid if there is another war. I would jump into the Lim, so that I do not see what I saw before.

To tell you the truth, it was my fate to live so long—fate at work. I would like my children to live long and to be healthy. But it is no good for a woman to live longer than 80 years. She cannot do anything. Look at me! I am no good to anyone. I cannot give anyone a hand or do anything. That is not good. No good!

If I were able to fulfill one wish for you, what would it be?

Even if I could go back in time, I would work as much as I could with my hands. But in the last five or six years my hands have given up. I would always think of my children.

Would I want to go to school? Oh God, would I! There were schools when I was young, but only three girls attended. We were too poor.

Thank you for sharing your life with us.

I Bog sinu i tebe dao zdravlje i sreču [And God grant your son and you good health and good fortune].

PART 4

We Are Sisters All

Without a word of warning to anyone
My mother died.

She did not want to bother anyone,
The world had enough problems and worries of its own,
She wondered off, so to speak, on tiptoe.

And since then, I have been more caring of old people,
I give them my seat on a train, on the bus,
Sometimes I feel like taking them into my arms like children.

Even when I don't know them, I talk to them, smile idiomatically.
In winter I am afraid they will catch a chill or a cough.
I always avoid the obituaries.

I have the impression that some day
A letter from afar will fall into my hands
'How are you doing? How are the others?'

Without leaving her address
She continues to wander on tiptoe
Amidst the din of the world, its pain and lamentation.
—Rudolph Marku, "In Memory of My Mother"

The ancestors of the three Albanian women in this section, Muslim and Roman Catholic, inhabited the land on which the centenarians now live. Prior to the Balkan Wars, this land was part of northern Albania. Following the wars, it was annexed by Montenegro. Because the inhabitants were not uprooted from their ancestral land, they did not have to make too many adaptations, except that this partition separated them from some family members in other areas of Albania. As citizens of Montenegro, they were free to practice their individual religions without threat of repercussions. Albanian society was as much a patriarchy as was the new country. Moreover, Albanians were not the *first* Muslims on Montenegrin soil.

Not unlike Albanian Muslims, many Slavs converted to Islam more than 500 years ago, after the occupation by the Ottoman Empire. Although I made numerous attempts to interview Slavic Muslims, I did not succeed. Several Muslims came forth with names of women in the Sandjak region of Montenegro, an area in the north with a large concentration of Slavic Muslims, but the women failed to materialize. It would have been interesting to hear their stories of life in a land that was perpetually at war with people of the same nationality, separated only by religion. Many retained the suffix of their Slavic surnames, adding an Islamic prefix and given name, for instance: Ahmet Sultan*ović* and Azra Alibeg*ović*. For this reason and for their Slavic physiognomy, these Muslims are readily identifiable. Having the identical patriarchal history as other Montenegrins, they have preserved several pre-

Islamic, Christian traditions, such as monogamy. The Koran condones polyg-
amy, but Slavic Muslims do not maintain harems. In the time I spent in the
region, there was not even a remote hint of religious intolerance or prejudice
on either the Muslim or Christian side.

Excluding religion and its associated traditions, one would be hard-pressed
to note any discernable distinctions between the patriarchal practices of Montenegrin Eastern Orthodox Christians, Slavic Muslims, Albanian Muslims,
and Albanian Roman Catholics. Whether or not this evolved intentionally
is beyond my grasp. Had Montenegro exerted pressure on Catholics and
Muslims to convert to Orthodoxy, no visible sign of Roman Catholic
churches and Islamic mosques would have remained. That is not the case.
Churches and mosques proliferate. What is clear is that the manifestly circumscribed patriarchal structure of Montenegro has enveloped all those who
live within its borders. The narrated autobiographies of the following three
Albanian women testify to the collective experience of all women in Montenegro.

FATIMA

Fatima, a slight, 103-year-old woman, lives on the Adriatic Coast with her son and grandson and their wives. She is an Albanian Muslim who wears a white kerchief on her head in addition to the traditional *dimije* [pantaloons] made of printed fabric. The house is in pristine condition, both inside and outside. The garden consists of a well-maintained grape arbor interspersed with magnificent flowers, already in full bloom although it is early April. It is one of those warm, bright spring days in Montenegro. After my coordinator and I are introduced to members of the family, her daughter-in-law and her grandson's wife serve fruit juice [alcohol is prohibited by the Koran], *lokum* [a sweet candy], coffee, cheese, yogurt, and fresh bread to their husbands, my coordinator, and me. Fatima's daughter-in-law also wears traditional Muslim dress, whereas the younger woman wears modern clothing.

I conduct the interview in a private room, to which Fatima and I are directed. Despite her advanced age, she needs no assistance in walking. On one wall in the room hangs a *ćilim*. Another *ćilim* covers the couch on which Fatima sits. From my observation, I note that Muslims decorate their homes in considerably brighter colors than non-Muslims, particularly in urban areas. Fatima responds to my questions in the manner to which I have become accustomed: clearly and fluidly, without inhibition. She often adjusts her head scarf, making certain that every hair is covered. When I take her picture, I half-expect her to attempt to cover her face, but she never makes the slightest effort to do so. As a young woman, she undoubtedly wore a veil over her face until the tradition was abolished by Tito in 1945. Even when we go into her beautiful garden for additional photos, she is most cooperative. When the time comes to depart, I thank her for the interview, and we embrace warmly.

Fatima's grandson's wife drives the coordinator and me to the railroad station. I miss the train by several minutes, but it does not present a problem. My coordinator lives in the area, and we use the time between trains to visit the home of his friends, a Montenegrin family, where we are welcomed with traditional hospitality and interesting, free-flowing conversation.

In this popular tourist city, women, including Muslims, have significantly more opportunity for exposure to the public, both native and foreign, than those in rural areas. Such social interaction encourages a greater degree of openness. This is true, more or less, of all coastal towns.

Zorka: Talk to me about your early life in your natal village.

Fatima: What could I tell you about it? It was a very difficult life, *moja* [my dear]. Terribly difficult. We had nothing, *moja*. We all had to work as children. We knitted and weaved a lot. We made cornbread, cooked potatoes and beans. Even if you had money, there was nothing to buy. *E, ja* ["Oh, yes"—an expression accompanied by a deep sigh].

Was your marriage arranged?

E, ja. Someone comes to ask for your hand in marriage. That is the way they were with women. I was married in another village. I really cannot remember how old I was when I got married. I do not want to lie to you. That would be a disgrace.

I never saw my husband before the wedding. I saw him for the first time when I went to his house to get married. I never saw him before that. Never! Of course, I was not afraid. Not at all.

[She laughs.] It would have been stupid if I told my father I did not want to marry the person he picked out for me. "I do not want him." Never! That would have been stupid. They would not even hear you. The job is over. Once it is done, it is done forever.

Did you ever kiss a man before you met your husband?

Kiss a man before I was married? God forbid! Only my husband, and that was after we were married. Not with anyone else. No, no, only my husband!

What was your wedding like?

There was lots of food: meat, *pilav* [a rice dish], soup, bread. That is the way it was in those times. We first went to the *djamija* [mosque]. We did. Yes, we did. Then, after the ceremony in the *djamija*, we went to his house. I was dressed like every other bride, all in white clothing. [Muslim brides wear white.]

I found two brothers-in-law in the house. No one else. No mother-in-law, no father-in-law. Just my husband and his two brothers. There were three. Three brothers. His parents had died, and only those three were left.

Did you sleep with your brothers-in-law before you slept with your husband?

Oh God, no! That is only a custom among Montenegrins, not with us. We sleep only with our husbands. It is not our custom for the bride to sleep

112

with her brother-in-law on her wedding night. You slept with your husband. We even had a separate room, a room for ourselves. They slept in their room, and we slept in ours. That is the way it was, *moja*. That way. I did love my husband, my God. He loved me, and I loved him. Sure, we kissed a lot. I do not know if I lived this long because I lived with a man who loved me, and I loved him. He died a long time ago. He died 40 years ago.

Tell me about your children.

I had six children—three boys and three girls. It does not matter if you have boys or girls. They are the same. Yours is yours, *moja*. Oh, yes. It was much better to have sons in this society. They liked them more, much more than girls. The men fire their guns when a son is born. Everybody is happy, especially the men. But so are the women.

There were no hospitals at that time, *moja*. No, no. I had them all at home. Oh, yes. I had them all in bed. [This meant she had them in the house, but not necessarily in the bed in which she and her husband slept.] And life was so difficult. There was nothing, nothing.

Some women gave birth all by themselves, but usually you find some woman who holds the baby [as it exits the body], then she settles it and diapers it. There is always a lot of pain. Oh, no, my husband did not hear me. He was a strong man and young, so he slept well. He did not hear a thing.

I breast-fed all my children. That is what we do. Some I breast-fed for a year, some a year and a half.

What? My husband and I decide on how many children we should have? No, no! We never decided on anything, only what God wrote down. You have—you have. You do not have—you do not have. *Bogu hvala* [Thanks be to God]. Even if males are more important in this place, they are both loved the same, *moja*. You cannot separate the two, at least a mother cannot. Which finger can you cut off? They are all the same. Which finger can you cut off your hand? That is your own heart, *moja*. Of course it is known that males live better than females. Women take care of males. They are to be respected. First a woman looks after the males. Females learn very early to take care of themselves. They have to take care of others. There is no time for her. Every woman knows that. Even today women take care of the family.

What happened to children who were born physically or mentally disabled?

Of course some people had children who were not healthy, mentally or physically. What could you do? That is the way God made him, *moja*. You cannot kill it. No. But it did happen among some people. Yes, it happened.

That is very painful. It is painful to kill your own child. I do know of some situations where the mother killed her child. But they are stupid people. Stupid! They are stupid! So stupid! She strangles it when she is at work in the fields. She does not know what to do with it, so she kills it. That is the way it happened, *moja*. That is the way it was.

What happens if a woman is infertile?

When a woman could not have children in my time, the husband often just took another wife. He just takes another one. He keeps the first one, too. She becomes their *sluga* [servant]. She waits on them. She does all the work. That happened to my brother. [She laughs.] His wife could not have children, so he took another. He married her, kept her, and with her had six or seven children. The first one took care of them, and then she died. This one is still living. Her three sons are in America. And she has a son and daughter here.

He usually never sends an infertile wife back to her parents. He just keeps her as a *sluga*. Of course he sleeps with both wives. He spends the night sometimes with her, then her, or with both wives in the same bed. That is the way they did it, *moja*. That is what I heard. Yes. Not easy. My God, how could it have been easy? Then again, sometimes the wife has only daughters, which is also not so good here. But he keeps her anyway. What can he do when God did not give him a son? Sons are important. Especially here.

Yes, it happened that when the second wife has no children, he takes a third one. [She laughs.] They all remain in the house. And these are not big houses. Mostly one room. That is all stupid, *dušo* [a variation of *duša*, or soul].

Did some people marry outside of their religion?

Sometimes a Muslim girl would marry a Christian boy, and the parents are forced to accept it. The parents have no reason to get angry. That is their fate. Whatever happens is fate. What can you do about it? Nothing. But, still, they do get angry. Sometimes such a girl would be killed. Oh, yes. Many times it happened here. It is hard on the parents, especially when a son marries outside of his religion. It is hard with a girl, too, but it is much harder with a boy.

What would happen to an unfaithful wife, or if an unmarried girl had sex?

An unmarried girl get pregnant? God save me from such a thing! We call that kind of girl a *kurva* [slut]. It certainly did happen. When that happens some parents accept her, and some throw her out. Some take her, others do not. That is a terrible disgrace for the whole family. She blackens their names. She blackens her brother's cheek. What else do you live for but for this? [She pats her face.] What shame! What horror! One lives for this. What does one have but a name? What does one have but this [face]? One lives for this, *dušo*—for this. You have to be very careful. Control yourself. Control yourself.

It is just as bad if a married woman is unfaithful. That, too, is difficult. That hurts. That hurts a lot. I do not know how to tell you what her husband does to her. Oh, God forbid! Of course, we heard of it happening. She is stupid, *moja*. Some husbands keep her, and others throw her out. Some keep beating her, if he decides to keep her. Her life is not easy. She disgraced her husband and her family. It should not be easy for her. Sometimes the husband kills her. He usually hangs her. There was a girl who was engaged over there. She made a mistake by being unfaithful. Her family hanged her. Her parents hanged her. They are all stupid, *moja*. Oh yes, her parents hanged her over there. They hanged her. Her own parents did it!

What are funerals like here?

My husband died a long time ago. We were married for 50 or 60 years. He died of a stroke. What a pity! He died at home, and I was there when it happened. No, no! I did not scratch my face for him. I just grieved. Nothing else. Muslim women never go to the cemetery, so we are not there when they bury them. Only males go. They put a *čefu* [white skull cap] on the dead man's head, wrap him in a white shirt, and into the coffin with him, then into the grave. Nothing else is placed in the grave. They bury the body as soon as possible, though they keep it a little longer today. But in the old days they buried him right away. As soon as he dies, he gets buried. Quickly.

Is there a difference between the customs of Montenegrin and Muslim women?

There is no difference between the two. We all pray to one God. God created us the same. All the same, so there should not be any difference.

We worked just as hard as the Montenegrin women. We worked outdoors. We dug, we plowed, planted tomatoes and potatoes. We did all that work. No one did it for us. We were not like some Muslim women who live inside the house, sitting at home and taking care of themselves, oiling their skins and doing other things to look good for themselves and their husbands. Oh no, we never did that. We had to work so we could live, *moja*. We did not even have a dress to put on, forgive me. Today, they have enough to change their shoes and clothes five times a day. In my time, we had nothing. Forgive me, we would wash our children, wrap them in something, and put them in the cradle. Then we had to wait for his only change of clothing to dry so we could dress him. We were very poor. Today you could never find something like that happening in this country.

No one lived well in this land. Everyone was poor. It did not matter what your religion was. We all lived the same. Everybody suffered. Especially the women.

Muslim men, like Montenegrin men, had only one wife. [Muslims in Montenegro, those who converted from Christianity to Islam, remain monogamous, predominantly.] One wife, *moja*. We did not have harems here. Oh, some men took a few wives, but that was very rare. It is enough to support one and the children. Even that is too much sometimes. Today is much different. Can you imagine what it was like when I was young? Poor, *moja*. Poor. But even today, when there is much more, men only take one wife.

Do you remember the wars?

Of course. I remember the Turkish wars. I was married during the Turkish war—the Balkan war. My husband was a soldier in that war. I remember many wars. So many. In my lifetime, I lived through the Balkan Wars, then with the Austrians [World War I], then this one with the Italians and the Germans [World War II], and, finally, the partisans [a civil war fought during World War II between Tito's communist partisans and guerilla forces loyal to the monarchy].

All the wars were difficult, but this last one with the partisans was the worst. *E, ja,* the worst! The worst, *e, ja!* There was a lot of hunger. We were never hungry. There was always bread. As long as there is bread, you are not hungry. The soldiers were hungry. They had bread to eat, but nothing else. Nothing else. They lived through horrors. Soldiers need more than bread to fight. But they did. An only son [a neighbor's son] died over there during the war [in the civil war during World War II], *jedinac u majku* [the only son in his mother]. Eeeeee, he died over there. How would it not be difficult to lose your only son. Only son! Only son! An only son! Eeeeee!

How do you explain your longevity?

I do not know why I have lived so long. What can I do? We live as long as God says we should. We do not decide. He decides. Until God says, you live or die.

If I could offer you a wish, what would you wish for?

I have nothing to ask for. I have everything a *duša* would want. Whatever a *duša* asks for, I have. Here they are [her daughter-in-law and her grandson's wife]. They take care of me too well. Bless them. Two *nevjeste* ["brides"— it is not uncommon for a woman to be called *nevjesta*—a term of both endearment and respect—all of her life]. This is my *nevjesta* from my grandson, this one, *e, ja*. The other one is my son's bride. May God help them. Everything is good. Of course I would like to be young again, yes, yes, but only let it be the way it was.

Thank you.

Srečna i zdrava bila. Oprosti. [May you have good fortune and good health. Forgive me (used as an expression of modesty).]

PASKA

At 102, Paska is a handsome Catholic Albanian woman who lives in a predominantly Albanian village, situated near Lake Scutari, a lake shared by Montenegro and Albania. From her home the lake is clearly visible. She is introduced to me by a young attorney and university professor, himself a Catholic Albanian. He speaks fluent Albanian, Serbo-Croatian, and English, having studied in the United States. On our way to her house, we take a side trip to the village of his birth and his early years, prior to moving to Podgorica, where he currently lives with his wife and where he teaches.

I learn from him that it is only in the last 20 years that Albanians in Montenegro emerged into modern times, following centuries of backwardness and deprivation. In other words, Paska's grandmother's life cannot be differentiated from that of my coordinator's mother, born well into the twentieth century. Nor is there any disparity between his early years and those of his great-granduncles. He attributes his generation's extrication from such archaic conditions to the United States. Many of the Albanians who emigrated to America within the last 20 years have become financially successful. Their monetary support has helped their families in Montenegro to abandon the ancient villages for the larger cities and civilization. Within a couple of decades, they have built substantial homes and developed large tracts of land, which, with the aid of modern farm machinery, yield profitable agricultural products.

Among the numerous historical sites we visit is an imposing, seemingly isolated, Roman Catholic church, still in use by the local Catholic Albanians. Perhaps the most intriguing site is a vacant field, once an ancient burial ground of the Bogomils—an ascetic, heretical Christian sect, formed by a Bulgarian monk in the tenth century. A vast number of Bogomils settled in Bosnia. Nothing more was heard of them following their absorption into the Ottoman Empire during the fifteenth century, through conversion to Islam.

In Montenegro it is not rare to find two adjacent houses, one hundreds of years old, the other a relatively modern structure, built after World War II. The old house, now used as a shed or barn, is the type in which my narrators were married and spent most of their lives. We arrive in Paska's village. I find her now in the newer house, where she lives with her married great-grandson and his wife. We are greeted and welcomed by the young couple. Since the day is fairly warm and sunny, we enjoy a soft drink and pleasant conversation on the veranda. The young woman then leads me into the house, up to the second floor and into a bedroom. Sitting in a chair is an elderly woman, smiling as I enter. I immediately know that she is Paska, though her appearance belies her advanced age.

When Paska greets me in Albanian, a language I neither speak nor understand, I become rather anxious. The beautiful young woman in her early 20s assuages my fears by acting as translator. She is multilingual, having lived in Germany for most of her life, where her parents are *gastarbeiters* [guest workers]. She translates my questions from Serbo-Croatian into Albanian for Paska, then renders the Albanian responses into Serbo-Croatian for me.

When replying to rather personal questions, Paska is somewhat embarrassed in the presence of the young woman, though not deterred. Admittedly, I am just as uncomfortable. Paska is forthright in trying to provide as complete a picture of her life as possible. Some of the more intimate questions bring a smile to the young woman's face as she translates them. On hearing them, Paska, too, grins shyly, but never once fails to respond. What could have been an arduous and interminable interview was a pleasant experience because of the graciousness of both women.

Zorka: Tell me something about your life before you were married, when you lived with your parents.

Paska: There were 10 children in my family—six sisters and four brothers. All my sisters died. They died a year or two after they married. We do not know from what they died. There must have been some illness, seeing that only one sister lived—me. About 20 people lived in my house—my father and mother, 10 children, an uncle, and my father's sister. Twenty people in one house, in one room. I was the youngest of them all. Because all my sisters died, my parents loved me very much.

My mother was an only child. So, after she got married, her parents were left alone. My mother used to cry a lot for her parents because they were alone. Here, when a girl marries she goes to her husband's village and his home. She was so sad that my father asked her, "What is the matter with you? Do you miss your parents?" "Yes," she said, "I would like to give my son to my parents. They argue a lot, and if I gave them a child, they would not have time to argue. They would have to wash and take care of the child." Then, my father said to my mother, "So you are not sad and do not cry anymore, we'll give them the child." He was my eldest brother and their first child. Later, my mother had three sons and many daughters. Here people do not pay much attention to daughters. Sons are important. My parents were lucky; they had four sons, if you count the one they gave away. Four sons! Just what every parent wants.

My grandmother was not Albanian. She was a Montenegrin from Podgorica. I know that she was not young when she got married. But it did not matter that she was not Albanian. If you are Montenegrin or Albanian, you suffer. Life is hard here. We used to raise cows and pigs. So we always had milk and cheese, but not much else. Take a look around. Poor. Very poor. All rocks. Wherever you look, rocks. You cannot grow much on rocks. We live in a tough land, and we are tough people. The ones who are not tough do not live.

No, I did not see my brother very often. In this land there is no time to visit. Besides, we always leave our *rod* behind when we marry. And our *dom* is not always too near. Unless your birth family comes to see you, you never see them.

Tell me how you met your husband, and something about your engagement.

I was 17 when I got married. My husband had no one, no mother, no father—only two sisters in Albania. He was about 27 when we got married. He had just come home from the war [Balkan Wars]. I never saw him before we were married. They just gave me to him. My father asked him for 20 dinars, the price of a ring or a bracelet. Imagine! He gave me for so little. At that time all my sisters were married.

The oldest married first. My sisters did not know their husbands either. They only knew their fathers-in-law, because they were the ones who came to the house to ask for their hands in marriage. Nothing about the girl was important in those days except if she came from a good house. If he was from a good house, he could get a beautiful woman.

Could you have refused to marry the man your family chose for you?

Refuse? Refuse the man your parents picked for you? Never! Oh, no! We could never refuse the man our parents picked out for us. No one would dare refuse. That was a big disgrace. Whatever they decided for you, you did. Imagine refusing! They would have killed me, or at least beat me. In the end, I would have to take him anyway. So why cause trouble for yourself? Take it and live with it. After I had my child I spent a week with my parents. I rarely saw them after that.

Did you have a large wedding?

It was a fairly large wedding. We were very poor, so we could not afford much. I did not know my husband until I was brought to his house. I did not have children until four years later. Four years!

He lived all alone, and when they left me there I was so frightened that I

120

shook all over. [She begins to shiver and shake to show me how she felt. Even while she demonstrated, she is visibly frightened, as if reliving her wedding night.] I especially shook when I got into bed with him. Can you imagine how it was? You are with someone you do not know, never saw before. He asked me, "Why are you shaking?" And I said, "Oh, for no reason. I do not know why." And he said to me, "You do not have to be afraid."

He loved me, but he was very strict. Yes, he hit me a little. He hit me because of some word I said, or I did something he did not like. He did not allow me to go to church or to go shopping. I never went to the *pijac* [marketplace]. He was very jealous. He used to say, "When they see you, they will come to you. If you stay home, they will not come." No one ever came to my house. He hid me, so men did not see me. I have to tell you this, even though I am ashamed. My husband used to tie me to something in the house so that I could not go out. You can see that we do not have neighbors close by. Where would I go? He would not come home all day or all night. He gave me just enough room to move around. That is how jealous he was. See how I lived? Whatever he wanted to do, he did. Even if I could get away, where would I go? To my parents? Never! They would send me back, and my life would be even more miserable. So you suffer. That is what I did—suffer.

My husband had many other women in the village, so he never came to me [never had sex with her]. Of course there were those kinds of women in the village. He went to married women, those that had children. That is what men did. It was safer to go to a married woman. There were none of the houses [of prostitution], so men went to married women with children. If she got pregnant, she could always say the child is her husband's.

Didn't you complain to your husband about his treatment of you?

Complain? Never! How could I complain to him? I would not dare. Sometimes I did, and he would hit me. For four years he never came to me. People began to think that I could not have children. That is very bad. People marry to have children. I was ashamed, but I could not tell anyone about it. How could I tell them that my husband has not come near me for four years? They would not even believe me. They just thought that I could not have children. Women who cannot have children are not treated too well. So, after four years, when I saw that he is never going to come to me, I begged him, because I wanted children. He was happy doing what he always did, going to other women, but he knew that I was right. Then I began having children, but I did not have luck. I lost my first son when he was a child and the second one when he was a grown man.

How many children did you have, and where were they born?

I had three daughters and two sons. I gave birth to my son [first son] alone in the house. Well, I had him in the barn on some straw. Only God helped me. I struggled so much. Sometimes I would kneel down to give birth, sometimes I would lie down. There were no doctors then. I had pains for 12 hours. My husband was home at that time, but he did not help me. He just lit the fire. I had a difficult time getting up to wash the baby. I thought I was going to die. He was upstairs and I was downstairs in the barn. You know the way our houses are. People live on the top floor, animals on the ground floor. We did not have any warm clothes either, and it was winter. I do not know how we survived. I suffered too much. All my children were born the same way.

My husband was very happy when he learned he had a son. He did not fire his gun, but relatives from the village came and fired their guns. When I had my second son, they fired less. They said, "Now, they will have many."

Two of my daughters died when they were very little. One lived for five weeks, the other for a half-year. Also, one of my sons died when he was little. Having a daughter is not too good, but having more than one is even worse. This is especially true in homes where there are no sons. I know of a husband who said to his wife who just gave birth to a girl, "If you have one more girl, I will kill you." He really does not kill her, but they argue a lot. They keep trying very hard to have a son. No one in this country is happy having daughters, not even mothers. This is not a place for girls— only boys. That is what everyone wants. That is what makes everyone happy.

Many women nursed their children for a long time. This was true with women who were not honorable. They did not want to have many children. As long as she nursed, she did not get pregnant. [Wives who used any form of birth control were considered undesirable and worthless, even by other women.]

What happened to an unfaithful wife or a girl who had premarital sex?

When an unmarried girl got pregnant, she was ridiculed by everyone. She could never associate with other women. That was a terrible disgrace for the father, brother, and everyone. Those bastard children were thrown in the garbage, as if nothing happened. Some of those girls committed suicide by jumping into a well. Sometimes she would drown the baby in the well. What is the sense of living when everyone curses you and beats you? The father of a bastard child was never killed, but no one went into that house again. It would have been better 50 or 60 years ago if they killed such a man, then it would not happen again.

An unfaithful wife was either killed or sent home to her parents, who did not want her either. And if her husband kept her, he would beat her every day of her life, and she could not do anything about it. She just had to take the beatings. What she did was not good for her or the family. Some disappeared. Some even killed themselves. It is better for her not to live. What she did is terrible. A disgrace!

It must have been difficult for you when you lost your children.

Losing any child is terrible, even if they are little. But the death of a son is the worst, the worst of all. There is no worse. My eldest son was murdered. There was some kind of argument concerning his sister's daughter. The girl was his niece. That is all he told me about it. All I know is that they killed him. [Most blood vendettas result from an insult to a female member of the family.] He was 52 years old. We wore black for three years, including a black scarf covering my head. I was not allowed to cry at the funeral. It was the custom that a mother cannot cry for her son, and she was not allowed to wear black. Everyone could, but not the father and mother. I wore black for three years. [Catholic Albanian women, like Montenegrin women, wore black when they were in mourning.]

Today people take food to the cemetery. That was not done when I was first married. Now they take *rakija* [brandy], cognac, and cigarettes. These are served to the men only, even though women are there. Women go to the cemetery, except among Muslims. After five weeks a priest comes and gives a service at the cemetery, and people serve wine and juice, and cookies for the children. Sometimes three brothers are buried in the same grave. Even four bodies could fit in there. It is like a cellar [crypt]. Each grave is a meter and a half deep.

I knew of a situation where someone was buried alive. [Bodies were not embalmed, and there was no doctor to pronounce death. The family or a villager made the determination.] Do you want me to tell you about it? There was a girl, around 15 or 20 years old. She lived a little farther away from here. She was chasing after some goats and fell into a well. [Some wells were at ground level and uncovered.] She was a Muslim. They found her, and the *hodja* [muslim cleric] came. They wrapped her in some rag, placed her in a grave, and buried her. Later on, people heard her crying. No, they did not dig her up, even though they heard cries. You know, Turks [meaning Muslim], they are buried in the ground. Who knows why they did not try to dig her up? We never had too much to do with Muslims. They have different customs.

Was there any hunger here?

During wars, especially the Turkish and Austrian wars, people were hungry. I have to say that when the Turks were here it was not bad. We had enough to eat. When the Turks left, they left behind as much as we needed. But when the Austrians came, we had nothing. We picked onions and some kind of grass, and they [the women] made some kind of bread. That is what we ate. Of course people died from hunger, many children and adults. The Turks left flour, so we were able to make bread. Because the flour was full of worms, we sang a song: "From those worms, we will burst!" And many people did die from those worms. I guess you cannot understand this. You are an American.

What was war like here?

My son's grandfather [her father-in-law] was in the war. He and my brother were killed. Everyone was trying to run away. The Turks wanted to destroy everything. Some people even gave their children Turkish names so they would not get killed. Even if they were Catholics, they gave them Turkish names. There were some Catholic people in my village who changed their names, and to this day they remain Turks. They do not go to the *djamija*, but they celebrate *Ramazan* [or Ramadan, the holiest period in Islam, lasting 40 days; people fast from sunrise to sunset]. They do not eat pork. Those people are my cousins; our fathers were brothers. Now, one is Catholic and the other a Turk. But we get along. We go to each other's weddings. We have the same things, except one is Catholic and the other is a Turk.

In my village two or three men killed about 28 Turks, but they ran out of ammunition, so the Turks killed *them*. The Turks took my grandfather. They offered him some coffee, and he said, "I am at war with you. We fought against each other, and I will not drink coffee with you." He was a brave man. All our men are.

Did you know some Turks used to cut off the heads of people? I never saw them do it, but we heard and knew it happened many times. As soon as we heard them coming, we would run and hide, leaving behind our houses, land, and everything we had. The Turks were not good. They did everything to us.

Were women raped during war?

That was the one thing women feared the most. The enemy always burned down houses, and women used to hide so they would not get caught by a soldier. You never saw a woman outside of her home. What a life! Either we had nothing to eat or our men were dying in wars. We were burying our children because we had nothing to give them when they were sick. And, on top of everything else, we had to hide so we would not be raped. You can see how difficult our lives were. Mine was no different from the others. Everyone suffers here.

Did you socialize much with other women in the village?

Socialize? Never. First of all, while my husband was alive, I could never go anywhere. I always stayed home. There was not time to socialize. I guess if I had a sister-in-law or a mother-in-law I could talk to her, but I had no one. No one. The only people I had around me were my two children. That is all. Just them. My husband was hardly ever home. Even when he was, he hardly spoke to me. I was alone, always. I told you I was never allowed to go to the *pijac*. So, I never had a chance to speak to other women. Women never spoke to men, anyway. But I would have liked to be with some people. And that is the way I passed my life. Now I am old and sick. It is too late for me.

If I could grant you one wish, what would it be?

Oh, if I could just have some medicine. That is most important to me. I am a diabetic. I have to get up about 30 times a night to go to the bathroom. I cannot sleep. I am so tired.

Thank you very much.

Živa bila [May you have a long life].

NADIRA

I interview Nadira on a Sunday morning when the Catholic Albanian population is attending church service; the streets are sparsely populated. Several hours later, there are throngs of people dressed in their Sunday best, walking up and down the main street, greeting one another, some stopping to chat. Men are sitting in the local cafés, smoking and drinking. The young, male and female, continue socializing on the street, while the older women go directly home, presumably to prepare dinner.

Nadira, a 102-year-old Albanian Muslim, lives near the center of the town, which is predominantly occupied by Albanians. My male coordinator escorts me into the house and introduces me to Nadira and her grandson and his wife. The men leave immediately. Such deportment is not surprising in a culture where women and men traditionally do not interact. Younger male and female Muslims, often university educated, wear Western clothing and loosely adhere to such practices in public. Whether they behave similarly in the privacy of their homes—that is to say freely—I have no knowledge. Following the civil war in Yugoslavia during the early 1940s, Tito, a communist and atheist, forbade the wearing of the veil by Muslim women. Some conventions nevertheless remain relatively intact, notably among the elderly.

In stark contrast to the solid black attire of Montenegrin women—except when they wear the national dress—Muslim women, regardless of age, prefer bright colors. Nadira wears *dimije*, a white blouse, and a large white scarf that covers her head and most of her forehead. We sit in what must serve as both a living and dining room during the day and a bedroom at night, a curtain separating it from a pristine kitchen. It is pleasantly furnished with a convertible couch, chairs, a dining-room table, and a television set. The young woman serves *lokum*, juice, and coffee while we chat. The interview takes place in an adjoining room, in which there are two couches and a wardrobe.

Although I had come to expect my interviewees to be verbal and forthright, I am also braced for the reverse eventuality, especially with Muslim women, who, I am told, are relatively reticent. I am proven wrong. Muslim women in Montenegro are responsive and candid. Without the slightest reluctance, Nadira responds to my every question. It is not until the end of the interview, when I want to take her picture, that I sense some resistance. While I ask her to look into the camera, she casually attempts to draw the ends of her scarf over her face. I wonder whether this is a vestige of the time, more than 45 years ago, when she wore a veil.

126

Zorka: What was life like with your natal family?

Nadira: I was born in a village where the old people lived—where they fought [wars], where they always fought. I lived there with my parents and brothers. My father was married twice. He had, my God, many children. His first wife died, and he took a wife from another town, a bigger town. With his first wife he had four children. One daughter died right after she married. This daughter was not married a year when she had a son, and then she died. My God, I do not know what she died from. She just had a baby and died.

He then married another woman, my mother, to take care of his children. And my mother raised those children. She loved them, and they loved her. In the old village, they all loved her. It is not like that now. Now, they cannot stand the sight of their mother. No, they cannot.

My mother had many children. She was also married before, and when she married my father, she brought two daughters with her. She was a widow. One of her daughters died before she married my father. With my father she had three children—two daughters and a son.

My grandfather took good care of his daughters. The poor man had no sons, so he took care of his daughters. It was not easy for him to have no sons, no one to carry on his name. That is very important here. My mother's father, mother, and sisters all died. She was left, but she did not live long. She was always sickly. This mother of mine was very sick.

My father treated my mother so-so. He was the way most men were in the old times. Men do not pay any attention to women. He only noticed her when she did something wrong. He never hit her, my God, never! But there was so much work to do. There were so many children to be fed and raised. It was not easy. He had to take care of the animals and the fields, so that we did not go hungry.

When we were little we went to school. We studied [the Koran, the Islamic bible] under the *hodja* [Muslim priest]. We did that only when we were little. As soon as we were old enough to work, we planted wheat and harvested it. We also removed kernels from the corn, and we milked the animals. In those days, that is the way it was.

How did you meet your husband?

I was about 18 years old when I got married. Eighteen years old. One of my sisters-in-law knew me, and she told my husband that I was a good girl, and she would marry me to him. That is how I got engaged. In our tradition we never pick who we are going to marry. That is all done by someone else. They choose someone for you. They never ask you. And you say nothing because they are your family, and you must respect your family. He was young, too. Maybe five or six years older.

Our families do everything to marry off their daughters, just so they can get them out of the house. That is what they really wanted—to get rid of the daughters. Daughters are not too welcome. Parents always have the worry of getting them honorably married. She goes away to her husband's village. Many women never see their families again. Sons stay home, married or not. Parents also try to get them married. The sooner they have children, the better. In this land, the sooner they have sons, the better. Pity the home that has no sons, like my grandfather. A pity!

Did you fall in love with your husband immediately?

Fall in love? Fall in love? We never even thought of such a thing. You went directly from one family to another. From your house to your husband's house. Kiss a man? God forbid! When we saw some member of a husband's family from a distance, we would cover our faces immediately. Then we ran as fast as we could, so we would not be seen. [She covers her face with her head scarf.] It was not a custom for us, then, to be seen by any member of the husband's family until we were brought into his house. My husband never saw me. He did not know what I looked like. I did not know what he looked like, either. Two strangers who have to spend the rest of their lives together. Imagine! Two strangers! My God, that is the way it was. But the people praised me. They said, "She is pretty, she is good, and she is a good homemaker." That is how they praised me. That is the way people got married in the old times. Good family. Good character was important. Most important.

My husband was in the army when the Austrians were here. His father wrote him that he wanted to arrange a marriage for him to this or that girl. He said to his father, "If it will please you, arrange an engagement for me." After we were married, I said to him, "How could you get engaged without seeing me?" He said, "My brother wrote to me that he is pleased with the girl" [his father chose]. No one asked me anything.

They [the husband's relatives] came to get me with a horse. In the olden days they carried the bride on a horse, while her two brothers-in-law held her hands, walking alongside the horse—one on each side, and the bride on the horse. They hold your hands to show you that they will protect you. Now you are one of their family. That is how I came to my home.

Tell me about your wedding.

During the wedding ceremony they tie the bride next to her husband. No, not because they were afraid she would run away. It was the custom. She belongs to him. Yes, my God, that is the truth. There was no singing. There were no musicians at that time, no, no. There was no music then. There was only firing of guns. Pistols. Lots of firing. Men like guns. They love to fire them. But no musicians.

We did not have much of a wedding. There were very few weddings, not like now. There was no *rakija*, no nothing. They did have rice, meat, soup, and pita. The kind of pita you make by stretching the dough very thin. Do you know what I mean? They fired guns on my wedding. My God, they fired a lot.

When I got to my husband's house, I found two brothers-in-law, a mother-in-law, and a sister-in-law. My mother-in-law had two or three daughters. One died and two were left. They loved me like these two eyes. Aoooooo! They loved me. When it got dark, my brother-in-law would protect me so that I was not afraid and to show me how much they liked me in the house. He would sit next to me. You are not afraid when they treat you that way, even if they are strangers. They were all strangers to me.

The house had two or three rooms, small rooms. It was an old house, God help you, small houses, small rooms. One room was the size of these two beds [she points to two sofabeds]. Of course I slept with my husband the first night. No, no, God no! Not with my brother-in-law! No, no! We did not do that. Now they go on a honeymoon. Sometimes they go away for 10 days before they go to the husband's house. No one ever did that in my time. Never! It was just like I told you. That way.

Oh, my God, of course I was afraid when I went to bed with my husband for the first time. A person is afraid of a strange man. Imagine, when you do not see him! You do not know him, my God, you are afraid. You shake like this [she begins to demonstrate with her hands how she shook]. This was my first time. And others, *jadne* [poor things], had the same thing happen to them. None of us know our husbands, and you sleep with a stranger—a stranger. That is how it was. Yes, he was good. I was not as much for him as he was for me. Every honor to him. Oh, the way he loved me! I gave birth to so many children, and he never said to me, "Woman, you gave me too many."

I brought a gift to my husband—a shirt and pants. We made everything. For my mother-in-law I brought a bracelet. That is what I brought. I also brought a nightgown and a comforter [made of goose feathers]. You do not know what that is, do you? Yes, and some pillows and a blanket made of wool—all of that.

You said you had many children.

Auuuuuuuuu! I had nine children—five sons and four daughters. One son died when he was little. He died suddenly, within a week. He was only a week old. And he was born big. You know, we Muslims have our children bathed by a *hodja*. When the *hodja* bathed him, he said, "I never saw a baby this size at this age." I dressed him and took him home. He died a few days later.

I gave birth to all of my children in the house. Not one was born in a hospital. We gave birth to our children in the house. [What she probably means is the bottom floor of the house, where the animals lived.] No one helped me when I was giving birth. My mother-in-law helped me with the first one. She loved me. I gave birth and raised them. Only God helped me. Then I gave birth again, and again, and again, again. One was born when the Italians were here. They were here for three years. That is when this one was born. He was born during the time of the [Communist] Party.

You were a much older woman when you had your last child.

Oh, yes, my God, I had plenty of years when I had this one. We were both old when we had this one, my God. Too old! [I heard story after story of women over 50 years of age having children.] A woman, a partisan, came into the house and said, "Are you resting?" They were fighting all around here, God help me, shooting all around. I said, "No, I am not resting, but I just gave birth." "How did you give birth when there is a war going on? War!" she said. "What can I do?" I said, my God. People were running into the mountains because they were afraid of the planes. Planes were coming from America, no, not America, but that other country. England, yes, England. The Germans told us not to be afraid. My husband spoke their language as well as they did. He said to me, "They are not throwing bombs here. This is a small place." My God, he was right. They did not bomb. Not even one bomb did they throw. No, my God.

My husband loved his daughters more than his sons. My daughter always used to say to me that she loved her father more than she loved me, because "you were not good to me." But I was good to them, my God. I said to her, "Now, when I do not see you for a month, it is as if I do not see you at all. But your father loved you all." That is what I said, my God.

When did you become a Muslim?

I cannot remember when we became Muslims. Oh, my God, that was a long time ago. A long time ago, when Mohammed was here [on earth], and he was a peasant. [The Ottoman Turks converted the Albanians to Islam in the sixteenth century.] At one time there were famous people here. No, He [Mohammed] will come back again. He will come back from the other world.

He has to come back. The way things are, no one listens to anyone. It is still that way.

We have been Muslims a long time, my God. Before that? Oh, God, we were never Catholic. Not Catholic! No! Mahomet [Mohammed] took one of yours for a wife. [She confused Mohammed with Sultan the Magnificent of the sixteenth century, who took as his second wife an Eastern Orthodox Christian woman from Belgrade, who became his favorite wife: "my love of another faith." He ruled during the period her ancestors became Muslims.] He took three wives, maybe more. [This is true of both Mohammed and Sultan the Magnificent.] I do not know how many. Our men take one wife. Maybe, some take more.

What happens to an infertile wife?

If a woman cannot have children, some of the husbands take another wife. Some men keep the first one in the house. A good man, a real man, does not get rid of her, like send her back to her parents. Her parents do not want her. Remember, I told you that parents can hardly wait to get their daughters out of the house. So she really has no place to go back to. No, he lets her stay in the house. Sometimes, some women will say to their husband, "Get married, so you can have a baby." My God, just that way. Women without children are very unhappy, and they feel sorry for their husband because they cannot give him any children. Children are very important. What is life without them? Empty. Some men kept two wives. The first one loved his children and took care of them like her own.

Of course he sleeps with both women if he wants to, and maybe if she wants to. He does whatever he wants. It is his wife and his house. Maybe the first wife will say to him, "Do not sleep with me anymore. You have slept with me long enough. Now sleep with that young one." She says that to him. One woman in our village, one of our relatives, married and had no children after I do not know how many years. Everyone in the village told her husband, "Get married, for God's sake, so you can have children." He got married, but he did not have any children with her either. So he kept both women without children. And he died. I do not know for how long he lived.

The two women were left without children. They now had property, and they both lived on that property, both, until they died. They left the property to some grandnephews they liked. You know, children from their brothers. My God, that is the way it was. They, my God, lived like single girls. God! God! They went from one house to another [visiting, something women generally did not do]. They went, they walked. No one interfered or forbade them to go. No, they went everywhere.

131

Are widows allowed to marry in-laws?

Of course. My God, a widow could marry her own brother-in-law. She takes her brother-in-law. She lives with him and maybe has a child or two. She takes her brother-in-law. She has children, and they love each other.

One woman over here in my village got married like that. With her first husband she had four sons and two daughters. Three sons are now in America. Then her husband died. Everyone was telling her, "Do not get married. You already have four sons and two daughters—six children—so do not get married." But she, my God, married her brother-in-law's son, her nephew. She married him, my God. He was like a child, young. She married him. She had property. She had her own property, and he married her. With him she had three sons and a daughter. *Ku Ku! Ku Ku!* [meaning horror of horrors] How could she have married him?

And there she is, still living. Alive! And her three sons and a daughter-in-law are all in America. Her husband died. Both of her husbands died. Only her children are living. She is now living with one of her sons here, and she has three daughters here, in Yugoslavia. Three sons in America and a daughter. That is how she got married. I am sure the families were not too happy about her marrying her nephew, but what could they do? She and he did what they wanted to do.

What happens to an unfaithful wife or to a single girl if she gets pregnant?

I do not know what happens when an unmarried girl gets pregnant. I do not know about that. She alone knows that. There. I certainly do not know about that. But, there are many, my God. There are many that are pregnant and not married. They raise them, I guess. I do not know whether any of them kills the child. That I cannot tell you. But some did get pregnant in the old times. They killed them in the old times. They wear some old rag around them, so no one sees them pregnant. In those times, that was a very bad thing to do. Everybody suffers. A big disgrace for everyone. Poor parents and brother!

It must have been very difficult for you during wartime.

There was fighting in the village where I was born. They fought with Crna Gora. My God, they all fought in the old times. That is the way it was. The Turkish country was here for 500 years. Five hundred! It [the Ottoman Empire] was in Sarajevo. It was in Bosnia. It was in Belgrade. It was everywhere. They always fought. Even the Muslim Albanians fought with the

Catholic Albanians! They all fought at one time. Now they get along. Now there is peace. Thank God, there is peace.

I lived through many wars: the Balkan Wars, the first big war [World War I], and then the second one with the Germans and Italians [World War II]. Then the civil war, when Tito was here. But, he [Tito] gave us freedom. He gave everyone freedom, and now they like each other as if they were brothers. He gave freedom. Everybody loved and respected him. Even czars and kings came to him. Of course I liked him. Why should I not like him? He made peace among the people. He brought peace to them all. You could walk everywhere at night. Even little children could walk around and not be afraid.

Before he gave us peace everyone was afraid of one another. We were afraid of those who always came to steal our cows and pigs. They even went into the old towns. They were the Catholics. They came around and wanted meat. Oh, no, God forbid. No, truly, the Muslims never did that, only the Catholics. That kind of Muslim I do not know. But, my God, the Catholics did. Yes, they did. They did.

The Montenegrins were very different. Montenegrin women were very good. They were sung about. In poems. Just to mention them was an honor. They sang about Montenegrin women who went to war. They carried guns, and it was a pleasure to see them go. Aaaaaa, I do like them. God help me, how can I not like them?

No, no, Muslim women did not go to war. Once they came to dress them up in uniforms. They dressed up my daughter, who is now in France. Some women came to teach them military things. That was during the partisan war. Then Tito gave everyone peace, and they were released. So they did not have to suffer anymore. Tito gave freedom.

You must have been very sad when your husband died.

Of course. I cried when my husband died. I did. I cried a lot. My daughter had died. I want to tell you about it. I had just married her. Her husband was desperate to become engaged. She was my second daughter. I have another one here in the village. And that went on and on. He keeps asking for her, keeps asking, keeps asking. And I do not want to give her to him. He was an only son, and then I began to think—he had animals, hogs, cows. I finally gave her to him.

She gave birth every year. In 12 years she had six children. Our custom is to circumcise. And she wants to circumcise three sons. She had four sons and two daughters, she did not want to circumcise the last son. First she said, "After my daughter marries, I will circumcise him." I do not know why she would say such a thing. She lived with her husband for 12 years. And then she drowned in water—my daughter drowned in water. She left behind three sons and two daughters when she drowned in that water.

I do not know how she drowned. I do not know if she did it herself. She was never afraid of water. So what happened to her we do not know. My husband used to say, "Do not tell them [the sons]." We had sons, so we did not want anything terrible going into them, so they wonder how their sister drowned [meaning that her suicide might be a bad omen for her brothers, should they know the circumstances of their sister's death]. My daughter's child was not even three days old when it died. She took the child with her. My daughter took her son with her when she died. Three sons remained. Her two daughters married and are now living in America. And that is it.

Women never go to the cemetery. Only men do that. But I have to tell you something as if you were my daughter. My grandson came to visit, and he said to me, "*Baba*, will you listen to me?" "For what?" I said. "To go to the cemetery with me, so you can see the grave," he said. So I listened to him, and I went with him, my son, and daughter-in-law. What are we going to see there? We are just going to see black earth, yes? We have nothing to see, my God. Nothing! Why people go to the cemetery I do not know. What good is seeing black earth?

Do people here practice blood revenge?

Of course there were men *u krv* ["in blood"—another expression for blood revenge]. They were *u krv* because that is the way it was fated. It is fated that they kill each other. Then they stop, and a year later they take *krv* again. Many men died that way. It goes on and on. Somebody says something to someone, insults someone in his family, and they are *u krv*. It is all fate—fate!

Did you ever hear that women were kidnapped?

There was very little taking of women. They would not dare. These *jadne* were never to show that they are alive, let alone make it possible for someone to steal them. Girls were afraid to go out of the house. There were some girls who liked to go out, but they were afraid their parents or brother would kill them. It happened in Albania. Well, in Albania there was a beautiful woman who wanted to go "on that road" [meaning to prostitute herself], and her brother wanted to kill her. So he took her away from that place, you know. And he wants to kill her, his sister. His other brother was alive then. He had two living brothers. One of his brothers heard that he did not kill their sister. He wondered, "Why did he not kill his sister?" So he went there and killed her himself. Of course he killed her, my God! She was a little wild. She wanted to go with Italians. So for that he killed her. He would not kill her for anything else. They had only that one sister. And there were three brothers. He killed her with a pistol, shot her until she died. That was a disgrace for your girl to go "on that road."

Does that also happen today?

That does not happen today, my God! Today they are educated! It is better that way. It is better she takes whoever she chooses than to fight, God forbid! He asks her, "Do you want me?" and she says, "Yes, I want you." He likes her, so he may have luck with her. Let him have luck with her, my God. What can we do? There, my son has had two [marriages]. I arranged the engagement of my three sons. They never once said to their mother or father, "With whom did you arrange my engagement?" They took who we picked for them. We did the best we could for them.

When you were young, did you or other women wear cosmetics?

Yes, my God. Women did take care of their skin. They protected their faces. Yes, yes. They were looked-after women. Truly, they were. There was something they removed their eyebrows with. I know you do not know what that is, but in the old days they did not have what they have today. They did not have pluckers [tweezers]. No, there was something they boiled. Like wax. They boiled it in a *djezva* [pot for making Turkish coffee]. Some old lady who knew how to do it would VAP! VAP! VAP! VAP! [she pats her face] Then again, VAP! over the face. Some women in the old times made things so that the face shines. So the face looks young. Some women had beautiful skin at 80 years of age. That is the way they took care of themselves. Even if they were poor, they found a way. They did, my God.

Of course, they took care of themselves so they looked good for their husbands. But what do I know? I only know that I worked hard and had no time for anything, especially myself. My God, we worked hard! Some women did take the hair off their legs, but I never did. I never had too much hair on my legs. True, true. Some women took the hair off their legs.

Yes, they took the hairs from here also [pointing to her pubic area]. Now something else came out that is rubbed on and removed, and the hair comes off [modern depilatories]. Removes all hair, all! An old woman, around 80 years old told me, "My daughter buys it for me. She buys it for me." In the olden days they had some kind of golden henna. They called it that. They boiled it in a *djezva*. Do you know what a *djezva* is? Something in which you make coffee and more. So they would cook it in that, then they would spread it over their bodies, and the hairs would come off. No, no, I never used what just came out [modern depilatories]. I removed my hairs with what we boiled in a *djezva*. What they have now comes out of a factory.

Today they use a brush, they say, and the hairs come off. That is what they say, my God.

Was there any hunger here?

Yes, we were hungry, my God. Most times we were not, because we always planted something. But one year God sent us a grasshopper [locusts]. Maybe you do not know what a grasshopper is. Oh, oh! It was like clouds, that is how many there were in the field. And they ate everything—wheat, tobacco, and barley—when it was young. They ate it all.

How do I know God sent that? That is—God always does good. After a while the people never saw him—the grasshopper. God sent a white bird. Those were white doves. White like snow. God sent these doves, and they gathered all the grasshoppers. Never, never, never in their lives did they ever see those grasshoppers again! Even if one came into the garden, he would eat everything up to the mountain—never, never, never again! The bird that God sent saved us from hunger. I guess you never heard of such a thing. In this land, everything happens. Things that nobody ever heard of. Only here. Grasshoppers! Imagine! Grasshoppers who eat everything!

So during that time people were hungry. The grasshopper ate everything, everything in the fields. Do you know that everything was closed for nine months [meaning the fields where the grasshoppers had eaten away all of the plants]? Some people in our family died, especially over there, over there in the Arab countries. [She may have used *family* as a generic term for Muslim.] Here, not many people died from hunger, but there was much suffering. There was little to eat.

Have you ever made a pilgrimage to Mecca?

I went to Mecca many years ago. My son was not born yet. When I arrived in Mecca, I told my friend [a woman with whom she traveled] that her daughter-in-law was going to have a baby. I learned that from a woman who was on the trip. She was such a good woman that I will never put her out of my mind. [Inference may be that Mecca is a place of magic; hence the woman had prophetic insight.]

I went to Mecca by bus. Airplanes? We had no airplanes. We never even heard of airplanes. We were in a bus, and it was nice. I did not even get a headache. We were two women traveling together. My brothers-in-law went to Mecca, too. My head never hurt, and I was many years old. We stayed for five or six weeks. We did. We came by bus. We slept in a room they gave us. They gave everyone a room, of course. We drank water from a mountain.

Water. It came, cold water from the mountain, and it would ice up. They brought ice and threw it in the water. And my head never hurt.

If you were given one wish, what would you wish for?

Aaaaaaaaaa, a wish? I would ask for my dead son to come back—to have him live. And also that daughter who left six children. That is what I would wish, my God—that. She left six children. They were all raised without a mother. And their father got married. He had five or six more sons and daughters. No, now I am old, my God. Now, I would like God to help me when I die. Now I do not need anyone. I will, if God permits, find them all over there [in the afterlife]. If God wills it. I cannot—I cannot help anyone now.

Thank you very much.

Bog te blagoslovio [God bless you].

Epilogue

After completing the interviews, I began to reflect on what I was to make of this study, how I was to place it into some understandable context, some historical perspective. Not being an anthropologist by profession, I knew that a scientific analysis would be both amateurish and presumptuous. Several ideas began ruminating in my mind, not the least of which was the effect of this investigation into Montenegro's tribal past on me: an American woman born thousands of miles from her ancestral roots, reared by a strong, often anguished mother determined to preserve her ethnic heritage yet aware that her children were immersed in what she perceived to be another, seriously flawed culture. I was also curious as to how the patriarchy had played itself out in modern Montenegro, particularly with regard to women. What vestiges of the traditional world have been retained? What has been discarded? Allow me, first, to deal with my less emotional, less introspective observations.

To me it seems that much of tribal Montenegro remains. The birth of a male child brings forth gunshots, even from apartment dwellers. It is not uncommon to see males firing weapons out of an apartment window announcing the birth of a son or the day of his baptismal. Female children are not received as ceremoniously, though one frequently sees young fathers taking their daughters for a walk. A father changing a diaper or wheeling a baby carriage is unheard of. Yet, in modern Montenegro, having a daughter does not appear to be the catastrophe it once was, or so it seems.

One glaring distinction between past and present is education for women. Modern Montenegrin women are more than literate, many earning the highest degrees in their respective fields. Among its Balkan neighbors, Montenegro has been in the forefront of the movement to educate its people, including the female population. In a land where education is a form of religion, where the written and spoken word are prized, even those who receive minimal schooling are *educated*, compared with many in considerably more advanced countries. It is no wonder that when the opportunity for a higher education presented itself on a grand scale, after World War II, Montenegrins, male and female alike, already inculcated with the importance of learning, readily availed themselves of the opportunity.

Female engineers, architects, physicians, academics, scientists, poets, and economists have proliferated since World War II. In that sense, women's lives today are profoundly different from those of the women who came before them; the modern woman may even have received an education at a university far from home and tradition. Paradoxically, however extensive her training, she can never erase from her psyche the schooling she acquired from her illiterate or semiliterate mother. Not Paris, Vienna, or New York could obliterate the value system imbedded in the marrow of every Montenegrin.

All children of Montenegrin heritage inside and outside of its borders are consigned the seemingly genetic propensity to perpetuate the morals and ethics of traditional Montenegro, creating in them simultaneous pride and concomitant guilt with even the slightest broach of propriety. Being a Montenegrin male or female has never been and can never be simple. The rigid demands of its society make no allowances for digression; to do so—one is constantly reminded—would destroy what has taken centuries of sacrifice and tragedy to preserve. No Montenegrin is allowed to take such a responsibility lightly.

An outside observer in Montenegro is not immediately struck by distinct gender-based behaviors, such as prevailing male superiority and female submissiveness. On closer scrutiny, the layers begin to peel off and the reality becomes apparent. Though wearing the latest fashions seen in large Western cities, the Montenegrin woman, university degrees aside, well traveled and aware of diverse cultures and traditions, cannot escape the society into which she was born and from which came her nourishment.

Not unlike her predecessors, she remains subservient to her husband and to other males. It is she who takes on the responsibility of housekeeping and child rearing, while also working outside of the home. Her professional status, which may be on par with that of her husband, has no bearing on her obligation to her traditional role as a woman. She refrains from engaging in any public reproach concerning her immediate or extended family. Not only has she inherited the verbal fluidity of her grandmothers, she also knows this very proclivity, championed among Montenegrins, must be bridled in the company of men. Where it concerns her husband and his family—her mother-in-law in particular—she continues to take a backseat, so to speak.

The Montenegrin son of today maintains the same reverence for mother and sister as did his forefathers. By and large people live in large cities, yet the son's obligations to his parents persists; they are his responsibility. On closer examination, however, it becomes clear that the responsibility largely falls to his wife—the unmitigated caregiver. He does little for the family except as overseer. His wife's compliance is, after all, a reflection of his ability to remain in control of his household.

Given the daily regimen of the average working Montenegrin woman, it is evident that the strengths of past generations of women have not been lost on her today. The workday commences at 7 A.M. and ends between 2 and 3 P.M. A married woman's day, however, begins long before then. Frequently arising well before dawn, she begins preparing the family dinner, often completing it on returning home in the afternoon or during her morning break. Apartment buildings are permeated with the pungent smells of sautéing onions and boiling cabbage or sauerkraut in the early morning hours—so much so that they became my alarm clock. She attends to breakfast and lunch for all members of the family, including in-laws; she lays out washed and ironed clothing for all; she cleans and polishes everyone's shoes.

After hearing an exhausted woman in a local supermarket reciting her daily activities, I suggested that her 13-year-old son relieve her of the task of polishing everyone's shoes. Shocked at what she had just heard, she replied, "What? A male polish shoes? My son? My husband would kill me even if I jokingly brought it up. No, of course he wouldn't hit me. But he would never allow his son to polish shoes. That would be demeaning and disgraceful for a Montenegrin. Remember, this is not America! Here, males young and old are treated as special people."

As the family exits the apartment in the morning, it is hard to believe that one person, who herself looks as if she has just stepped off the cover of a fashion magazine, could do all of this as well as hold down a full-time job— and do it without a word of anger. Or perhaps that is only the public image. What transpires behind closed doors remains there. Of course, one is invariably reminded that a woman's reputation is always at stake; she has no alternative but to accept societal mandates.

It is true that technology makes the modern Montenegrin woman's life physically easier than her grandmother's. Her apartment is centrally heated, with running water and indoor plumbing. Every home has a washing machine and other electrical appliances. A color television, a VCR, and a stereo are fixtures in the majority of homes, including those in some rural areas. All are a far cry from what were considered normal conditions a generation or so ago.

To a degree, today's Montenegrin is also emancipated in terms of personal relationships. Arranged marriages, in the traditional sense of the word, are not as prevalent, though they still exist in rural areas. Young people, principally those attending universities outside of Montenegro, have a greater opportunity to socialize than did their forebears. Those attending local universities cannot enjoy the same freedom. Even major cities are "villages," wherein a family name carries with it its entire history, a history familiar to all. The mere mention of my patronymic name elicited a litany of names and facts connected to that particular clan. I learned as much about my family from strangers as I did from relatives.

Though this society has become measurably freer, it still has some way to go to catch up with its Western counterparts. In most cases, families must approve of a young person's choice of mate. Parents continue to research the reputations of their children's future spouses. Dating is not commonly practiced, in the strict meaning of the word. A rigid sense of morality and family values remain firmly entrenched in the most liberated.

Premarital sex is no longer the shame it once was—for a few of the more liberated and rebellious young, or so I have been led to believe by some of them   but it is considered immoral by most people. Virginity for females is valued and expected. I heard from a number of sources that some young men are so fearful of marrying a nonvirgin that they select a future wife from among adolescent girls, and then, with the approval of her parents, watch over her until she becomes of marriageable age. Such occurrences would have been unthinkable and unnecessary in past years. As in the past, unwed mothers, of which there are relatively few, continue to be ostracized and are frequently forced to move to areas where they are unknown.

Is the adage "The more things change, the more they remain the same" an apt description of today's Montenegro? Yes and no—more yes than no. Excluding twentieth-century technology, embraced by Montenegrins wherever possible, culture and tradition prevail. A woman may be somewhat more socially vocal in the presence of males, but never to excess. Restraint in all situations continues to be her guidepost. My sense is that in the privacy of her home she, like her predecessors, "rules the roost," perhaps with less fear of reprisal from her husband, providing, of course, that she is ever-mindful of him as the embodiment of a glorious, tribal, warrior history—the preservation of which continues as the reason d'être for both. Only one born into and immersed in the culture can appreciate the pressure and pride inherent in being Montenegrin and the determination of parents everywhere to preserve their past.

To assume that patriarchal prescriptions are assigned to females exclusively or that females are the sole victims of its tenets would be a grave mistake. That modern Montenegrin women continue to take a secondary role to men and that they still enjoy the respect and protection of the entire society cannot be disputed. To a lesser degree, the Montenegrin male is also a victim of a carefully conceived society. He is required to behave as no less than a warrior and is treated as such. That is, at all times he must be fearless, honorable, and prepared to lay down his life for his name, family, clan, and, above all, the land.

He must never express disrespect for his or his wife's family. Should he do so, he would be considered a *ništa čovjek* (nothing man). He is expected to be articulate, to be well informed, and to engage in political discourse— a favorite diversion of Montenegrin men. He must walk erectly and proudly. Compassionate and tender, he shows affection for his nieces and nephews and other relatives—excluding his own children, though he loves them and they know he does. I suspect being affectionate in public toward those most loved is still considered a sign of weakness, of non-Montenegriness. Any public demonstration of affection for his wife remains unacceptable—a source of embarrassment for the entire family.

A noted psychiatrist told me that today's male is experiencing something of an identity crisis resulting from the diminution of specific masculine traditions: he does not ride a horse but drives a car; he does not carry a gun as part of his everyday attire; his wife is relatively emancipated. Notwithstanding this analysis, in which I suspect there is truth, the Montenegrin male must be ever-mindful of his behavior and what is expected of him. So must the Montenegrin female. Their public and private personas cannot deviate from the inherited text. They carry with them into the twenty-first century that which their ancestors bequeathed them: a set of clearly delineated guidelines for living as traditional Montenegrins—not a simple assignment, at best.

On a personal level, this study has taken me on an emotional journey. From early memory I recall my mother's stories of her life in *stari kraj* (the old country); her life seems little different from the lives of the old women I interviewed. While growing up, I wanted so badly for her to become "Americanized," to be more like the mothers of my Irish and German friends, not like those of my Italian and Jewish friends, who also were "foreign looking." I wanted her to speak English without an accent. Even as a young child I knew that was next to impossible, as long as we continued to live in close proximity to other Montenegrins. A "ghetto" existed wherever Montenegrins settled. Most other newly arrived ethnic groups had their communities as well, and their children no doubt had experiences similar to mine—the experiences of first-generation American children of immigrant parents.

I often speculated or perhaps fantasized as to how my mother would have changed had she lived among non-Montenegrins; the English, for instance. She never discouraged us from dressing discreetly in up-to-date fashions or from using cosmetics—a step toward assimilation she must have believed necessary. I always felt she was proud that her children were Americans, but she would have preferred us to be so on her terms—Americans with a healthy infusion of Montenegro. She frowned on dating and the openness of some Americans, especially women, which she considered unladylike. Women in her society did not laugh or speak loudly.

After the death of my father and our subsequent move to New York City, I thought, or rather hoped, my mother, now widowed and away from Montenegrins, would become a typically American mother, liberal and free from her native culture. That was not to be the case. She remained in contact with Montenegrins, with whom she naturally identified. They helped ease her loneliness and close the gap between her family in the old country and herself in America—something I was to understand only as an adult.

The fear of losing control over her children and having them meld completely into an American way of life compelled her, with a vengeance, to instill the values she deemed important for any civilized being—those same values with which she had been imbued and had brought with her across the sea. Her task was not an easy one. In a vast, alien, heterogeneous city, filled with incomprehensible temptations, how was my widowed young mother to impart to her children the rigid morality of her society? But she need not have been overly concerned, especially for those of us who were older; she had long since firmly imprinted on our psyches what it meant to be Montenegrin, including the guilt to sustain it.

Time mellowed her as she became comfortable with her surroundings. She became our most important teacher. She encouraged us to read and took us to the zoo, the movies, the botanical gardens, and the beach. We saw our first stage show in New York with her. These were her ways of introducing us to as much of American culture as she knew and thought important. As would any widowed mother in Montenegro, she kept alive the image of a strong, honorable, father-warrior for all her children, especially her sons.

As the oldest child, I was her prime pupil, the one expected to be the role model for the other children. All of my actions were monitored, at least those of which she was aware. Despite her admonitions, occasionally I managed to cut classes to hear the big bands and singers like Frank Sinatra and Doris Day at the Paramount and Strand theaters. I even ventured on a clandestine date or two. Though on a minimal scale, I was behaving like a self respecting American teenager. But that was no consolation, for I was continually plagued by feelings of guilt—by a conscience in the form of my mother, perched on my shoulder, overseeing my every move. She is there to this very day, I must admit.

As I stated earlier, it was not until much later in life, when I had married and become a mother myself, that I came to appreciate the battle my mother fought to instill in her children the values of an old culture. Intractability aside, her motives were valid and honorable. Relinquishing her identity and adopting one unfathomable and foreign would have unhinged and subsumed her and the offspring she was obligated to raise as moral and decent people. Otherwise, she would have failed as a Montenegrin mother. My siblings and I were informed and formulated by a culture determined to endure and a resolute mother who would see that it did just that. In the main, she succeeded.

On my return to the United States from Montenegro, I reviewed what I had experienced there and, more important, what I had learned. I had known about the dominance of males from the stories my mother told and from my parents' relationship with each other and with their Montenegrin friends and relatives. My father was a family man, and my mother tells me that he frequently expressed his joy in having a wife and children. In temperament he was quintessentially Montenegrin: reserved and fiercely independent. Being considerably older than my mother and a seasoned warrior of a traditional patriarchy (he had served in the army in the Balkan Wars and World War I), he ruled the household—albeit gently, yet we intuited when he was displeased. What he said was law and often impractical, but we loved him and were loved by him. He lived life on *his* terms, as did we as his family. My mother submitted to his wishes completely.

It was this portrait of the Montenegrin male that I carried with me—a portrayal profoundly incompatible with what I understood an American male to be. It was only after I completed the interviews and began to consider what I had learned from them that I understood my father—the embodiment of the Montenegrin male, spawned by a system reliant on strong, brave warriors for its preservation.

Montenegrins comfortably transplanted to America the love and respect they felt for their native land. They taught their American-born children to appreciate and honor a land that welcomed their parents and provided opportunities for a better quality of life.

When my narrators talked about their difficult lives and unending struggles to survive, I was not surprised. I knew all about their patriarchal land long before I ever set foot on it—this land called *Crna Gora,* Black Mountain, Montenegro, which I, from my earliest remembrances, knew to be mine also. In a strange way I had come full circle. I had come home to the land of my roots—roots bared by centenarian, illiterate, tribal women. Belonging to two worlds can be enriching.

Chronology of Wars and Conflicts in Montenegro

1042   Battle at Rumija against Byzantium (beginning of Zeta's independence from Byzantium).

1330   Battle of Velbužd against Bulgaria.

1370s   Battle of Spuž against Bosnian King Tvrtko I.

1380s   Prolonged and unsuccessful war for conquest of Kotor.

1418–1421   Battle against Venice for control of Skadar.

1423–1424   Zetan and Serbian forces fight against Venice over Skadar and Ulcinj.

1439   Feudal conflict in Zeta for control of Serbian Despotovina (rise of Crnojević dynasty).

1460   Continual battles with Turks (Ottoman Empire), who attempt to recapture eastern Zeta.

1470   Crnojević, in alliance with Venice, defends Skadar from Turkish onslaught.

1479   Crnojević, abandoned by Venice, fights Turks and loses (moves capital from Žabljak to Lovćen.

1487   Crnojević repels seven Turkish raids on Obod (Upper Zeta).

1604   Battle of Lješko Polje (Bishop Rufim and 400 highwaymen defeat Sandzak governor of Skadar).

1613   Battle at Kosovo Lug (near Danilovgrad) against Turks.

1649   Battle of Medun.

1685   Battle of Vrtijelica.

1690s   Intertribal conflicts.

1709   Christmas Eve Massacre of Montenegrin converts to Islam.

1711   Uprising of individual tribes against Turkish rule.

1712   Battle at Carev Laz (50,000 Turkish soldiers against 8,000 Montenegrins; Montenegrins are victorious).

1714   Raid on Cetinje by Numan Pasha Čuprilić of Bosnia (takes 4,000 Montenegrins to Bosnia).

1717   Battle of Trnjina (lasts seven hours; Turks are defeated).

1719   Battle near Nikšić (minor battle).

1721   Battle near Podgorica and Spuš (minor battle)

1725   Battle near Žabljak (minor battle).

1756   Battle of Prediše (Osman Pasha of Bosnia, with 40,000 soldiers, leads battle to capture Cetinje and is defeated after three hours).

1768   Turkish raid on Zeta by Bosnian Vezier Sulejman-pasha (defeated).

1785   Raid on Zeta by pasha of Skadar, aided by four "Islamized" Montenegrin tribes (take Cetinje but are forced to withdraw).

1796   Battles of Slatine and Krušima.

1805–1814   Periodic Montenegrin involvement in Napoleonic wars.

1819–1821   War with Turkey.

1828–1829   War with Turkey.

1832–1835   War with Turkey.

1847   Civil conflict.

1848–1849   Minor involvement in Revolutions of 1848 (revolt against Hapsburg rule).

1852–1853   War with Turkey.

1853–1856   Civil conflict.

1858   Battle of Grahovo (Turks defeated).

1862   Conflict with Turkey.

1874   Brief conflict with Turkey (no formal war).

1876–1878   Montenegrin participation in Russo-Turkish War.

1912–1913   First Balkan War.

1913   Second Balkan War.

1914–1918   World War I.

1918–1921   Civil conflict (Unionists, or "Whites," versus Separatists or "Greens").

1941–1945   World War II; Civil War (Communist Partisans versus Nationalist Četniks).

1991–1992   Yugoslav wars (Montenegrin participation in Dalmatian operations).

Pronunciation Guide and Glossary

Serbo-Croatian	Pronunciation
c	spats
č	lurch
ć	pitch
dj	injure
dž	gem
g	go
j	yellow
lj	cotillion
nj	onion
s	safe
š	sheep
ž	measure

Serbo-Croatian	Pronunciation	English
baba	baa-baa	grandmother, old lady
barjaktar	baar-yaak-taar	flag bearer
brat	braa-t	brother
čilim	chee-leem	handmade rug
čojstvo	ch-oy-stvoh	honor
Crna Gora	tsr-naa goh-raa	Montenegro, Black Mountain
Crnogorac	tsr-noh-goh-raats	Montenegrin male
Crnogorci	tsr-noh-gohr-tsee	Montenegrins
Crnogorka	tsr-noh-gohr-kaa	Montenegrin female
Crnogorke	tsr-noh-gohr-keh	Montenegrin females
dimije	dee-mee-jeh	pantaloons
djesni djever	dee-yes-nee dee-ye-ver	right-hand brother-in-law
djever	dee-yev-er	brother-in-law (husband's brother)
dom	dohm	husband's home, family
duša	doo-sha	soul
guslar	goose-lahr	man who plays the gusle
gusle	goose-leh	one-stringed musical instrument

jadna	yahd-nah	poor thing
jetrva	ye-tr-vaa	sister-in-law (husband's sister)
junaštvo	you-naa-sh-tvoh	bravery
kum	k-oo-m	godfather, best man
lijevi djever	lee-ye-vee dee-ve-yer	left-hand brother-in-law
lokum	loh-kumh	candy
nevjesta	nev-yes-taa	bride
opanke	oh-paan-kee	peasant shoes
oro	oh-roh	circle dance
pop	pohp	priest
privienac	pre-vee-je-naats	standard bearer
pršuta	pr-shu-tah	smoked ham
rakija	raa-kee-jah	brandy
rat	raa-t	war
rob	rohb	slave
rod	rohd	natal family
sin	seen	son
slava	slaa-vaa	patron saint's day
šlivovica	shlee-vooh-vee-tsaa	plum brandy
sluga	sloo-ga	servant
srecna ti rana	sre-ch-naa tee raa-naa	good luck with your wound
stari kraj	staa-ree k-raaj	old country
stari svat	staa-ree-s-vaat	wedding witnesses
stiditi	stee-dee-tee	to be shy, timid
Švabe	sh-vah-beh	Austrians
svatovi	svaa-toh-vee	wedding witnesses
tudja večera	tu-jaa veh-che-raa	a stranger's supper
tužbalica	tuush-baa-lee-tsaa	professional mourner
vladika	vlaa-dee-kaa	bishop
zaova	zaa-oo-vaa	sister-in-law (husband's sister)

References

Aleksandrov, A. "The Private Social Lives of Montenegrin Women." *Notes* (Cetinje) 12, no. 22 (December 1939): 370–80.

Baković, Todor. *The Depressive Optimism of Montenegrins.* Zagreb: Yugoart, 1985.

Boehm, Christopher. *Blood Revenge.* 2d ed. 1984. Reprint. Philadelphia: University of Pennsylvania Press, 1987.

Bogišić, V. *Sources Derived from Various Regions in the South.* Zagreb: Zupana, 1874.

Bojović, Jovan R., R. Jovanović, Z. Lakić, R. Pajović, and S. Stanišić. *Montenegrin Women in the Revolutionary Movement, 1918–1945.* Edited by Jovan R. Bojović. Titograd: History Institute of Montenegro, 1982.

Danilo I, Prince. *Prince Danilo's Legal Code.* Edited by Jovan P. Bojović. Titograd: History Institute of Montenegro, 1982.

Denton, William. *Montenegro: Its People and Their History.* London: Daldy Isbister, 1877.

Djilas, Milovan. *Land without Justice.* New York: Harcourt Brace, 1958.

Dragićević, Risto J. "The Girls' Institute in Cetinje." *Notes* (Cetinje) 4, nos. 4–6 (October–December 1949): 130–51.

Dragović, Ž. "Twenty-Year Report on Empress Maria's Girls' Institute in Cetinje." In *Montenegro,* 3–31. Cetinje: Montenegrin National Press, 1890.

Durham, Mary Edith. *High Albania.* Eastern Europe Collection Reprint. New York: Arno Press, 1971.

———. *Some Tribal Origins, Laws, and Customs of the Balkans.* London: George Allen & Unwin, 1928.

Filopović, Milenko S. *Among the People, Native Yugoslav Ethnography: Selected Writings of Milenko Filopovic.* Edited by E. A. Hammel et al. Ann Arbor: Michigan Slavic Publications, 1982.

Gezeman, Gerhard. *The Honor and Bravery of Old Montenegrins.* Translated from German to Serbian by Radosav Medenica. Cetinje: Obod, 1969.

Jovanovich, William. Preface. In *Njegoš: Poet, Prince, Bishop,* written by Milovan Djilas and introduced and translated by Michael P. Petrovich. New York: Harcourt, Brace & World, 1966.

Jovičević, Milan. *The Montenegrin Royal Marriages.* Translated by Hilda Zakraješek. Cetinje: Museums of Cetinje, 1988.

Kuzmanović, A. C., Dragoslav Srejović, and Olivera V. Žižić. *Classical Duklea: Hekropole.* Cetinje: Obod, 1975.

Laffan, R. G. D. *The Serbs: The Guardians at the Gate.* New York: Dorset Press, 1989.

Lord, Albert B. *The Singer of Tales.* Cambridge: Harvard University Press, 1960.

Marku, Rudolf. "In Memory of My Mother." In *Anthology of Modern Albanian Poetry,* edited and translated by Robert Elsie. Boston: Forest Books, 1993.

Medaković, G. "Crnogorka." In *Cultural and Legal History of Croatia,* edited by Ante Pukner, 65–73. Zagreb, 1882.

Miljanov, Marko. *Examples of Honor and Bravery.* Beograd: Čupić Foundation, 1901.

Nenadović, Ljubomir P. "About Montenegrins: Letters from Cetinje, 1888." *Notes* (Beograd) 3 (1929): 70–78.

Njegoš, P. P. *The Mountain Wreath.* Translated and edited by Vasa D. Mihailovich. Irvine, Calif.: Charles Schlacks, Jr., 1986.

Pajević, A. "A Portrait of the Lives of Women in Montenegro." *Memories of Montenegro and Hercegovina: Struggle for the Prelude to Liberation, 1876.* Novi Sad, 1981.

Pavlovich, Paul. *The Serbians: The Story of a People.* Toronto: Serbian Heritage Books, 1983.

Petrovich, Michael P. Introduction. *Njegoš: Poet, Prince, Bishop,* written by Milovan Djilas and translated by Michael P. Petrovich. New York: Harcourt Brace & World, 1966.

Rakočević, Novica. "The Situation on the Montenegrin-Turkish Border on the Eve of the Balkan War (1908–1912)." In *Istorijski Zapisi.* Cetinje: Obod, 1982.

Ražnatović, Novak. "Montenegro and the Congress of Berlin." In *Montenegro's Past,* edited by Dimo Vujović. Cetinje: Obod, 1979.

Saltzman, Alice Gibbon. "The Servants of Giants: A Study of the Role of Montenegrin Women over the Last One Hundred Years." Master's thesis. Antioch College, 1969.

Simić, Andrei. "Winners and Losers: Aging Yugoslavs in a Changing World." In *Life's Career—Aging: Cultural Variations on Growing Old,* edited by Barbara C. Myerhoff and Andrei Simić. Cross-Cultural Research and Methodology Series. Beverly Hills: Sage Publications, 1978.

Škerović, Nikola. "The Montenegrin Woman: Her Position and Her Duties in the Family." *Notes* (Cetinje) 4, no. 5 (May 1929): 257–64.

Treadway, John. *The Falcon and the Eagle: Montenegro and Austro-Hungary, 1908–1914.* West Lafayette, Ind.: Purdue University Press, 1983.

Vujačić, Vidak. *Ethos of Montenegrin Women: Traditional Behaviors of Montenegrin Women*. Titograd: Pobjeda, 1980.

Vukmanović, Jovan. "Crmnica: Anthrogeographic and Ethnological Problems." *Notes* (Beograd), 1988.

West, Rebecca. *Black Lamb and Grey Falcon: A Journey through Yugoslavia*. New York: Viking Press, 1941.

Index

The Author

Zorka Milich has a doctorate in English from St. John's University. She is associate professor at the State University of New York, Nassau Community College. She frequently lectures on her oral history research and on the writers William Faulkner and Ivo Andrić. She is a member of the Society of Woman Geographers and the Explorers Club. Milich and her son, Mark, and daughter, Andrea, are at work on a documentary film history of Montenegro and its centenarian women. She lives on Long Island with her husband, Wallace.